# STANDARD COSTS AND VARIANCE ANALYSIS

 **Institute of Management Accountants**

Certified
Management
Accountant
Program

## The Classics Series

IMA *Classics* are those Institute publications that have stood up well in the test of time. Published originally more than 10 years ago, these reprints are still "best-sellers" in that readers' demand for them continues. The reason lies in their contents; certain accounting principles and practices do not change.

*Published by*

## Institute of Management Accountants
(formerly National Association of Accountants;
founded 1919 as the National Association of Cost Accountants)

10 Paragon Drive
Montvale, NJ 07645-1760

Copyright © 1974 by National Association of Accountants
NAA Publication Number 7463
ISBN 0-86641-015-5

# FOREWORD

This publication brings together two NAA research reports which are now out of print: (1) No. 11-15, *How Standard Costs Are Being Used Currently* and (2) No. 22, *The Analysis of Manufacturing Cost Variances*. The former report contained the results of a study which were initially released in the NACA *Bulletin* (now MANAGEMENT ACCOUNTING). The latter report, originally published in 1952, supplemented the results of the study of standard costs. Hence, it seems appropriate to reissue both reports in one publication to meet the continuing demand by IMA members and others interested in practical applications of standard costing.

Part I comprises Chapters 1 through 5 of the former Research Reports 11-15. In it, Chapter 1 takes a broad view, covering the entire field of standard costs. The emphasis is on their uses, the ways in which the various uses are coordinated, and the principal problems which arise in developing and applying standard costs for each purpose.

Chapters 2, 3 and 4 describe practice in the use of standard costs for control of manufacturing costs, inventory costing, and pricing and budgeting. These chapters present the results of a field study conducted by the Association's research staff with participation of 72 companies employing standard costs. Each company's procedures were recorded and the underlying reasons were discussed. A partial list of these companies will be found on page 94. A review was also made of the many standard cost case studies which had been submitted for publication in the NACA *Bulletin* over a period of years.

Chapter 5 concludes the study of standard costs. It presents a case study to illustrate how one company makes full use of its standard costs and how these uses are coordinated. Professor Charles R. Scott, Jr., prepared materials for the case study report.

Part II deals with the analysis of manufacturing cost variances. It presents the results of a study designed to show what the accountant can do in providing management with information which will aid in appraising the significance of manufacturing cost variances. Managers of 27 companies employing standard costs were interviewed to determine how variances from standard costs are analyzed and what benefits are realized from such analyses. In addition, records of interviews carried out during the Association's field study of standard costs were drawn upon for material not released in the reports on standard costing.

The emphasis of the study reported in Part II was placed upon methods employed by those companies which were judged to be making most effective use of standard costs. For this reason, the report stresses practices and viewpoints of a comparatively small group of the companies interviewed. This approach was selected because it appeared likely that the most advanced practices would be more useful to members of the Association than those practices which were most commonly found. A partial list of companies which participated in the study is given on page 47 of this section.

Part II ends with an Appendix on computation of variances. It includes illustrations of two-variance methods in computing direct cost and overhead variances, as well as methods of developing three overhead variances.

# CONTENTS

# Part I

# STANDARD COSTS

Published originally as NAA Research Reports 11-15
*How Standard Costs Are Being Used Currently*

# Chapter 1

## A REEXAMINATION OF STANDARD COSTS

COSTS may be determined before the fact and after the fact. Both predetermined costs and actual [1] or historical costs have their place in modern industrial management. To take action or make an important decision without an estimate or predetermination of costs involved is to gamble or to speculate rather than to manage. Equally evident of lack of management is failure to determine the costs after the fact and to compare them with the advance estimates or standards.

Perhaps too much attention to cost "systems" and too little attention to cost uses has led to a lack of appreciation of the complementary roles which predetermined or standard costs on the one hand and actual or historical costs on the other hand can and should play in the management of industrial companies. As stated in an earlier N. A. C. A. research study, "Costs are used for a variety of purposes, and the same cost cannot serve all purposes equally well." [2] For some purposes historical costs are most useful, for others predetermined costs are needed, and for still others a comparison of the two serves management best.

The purpose of this chapter is to inquire into the various uses of standard costs, to question how well standard costs can serve these purposes, and to point out the areas of conflict and compromise which arise.

### Both Standard and Historical Costs Needed

While this study deals with standard costs, it is based upon the premise that such standards complement rather than replace actual costs. Actual or historical costs are an essential part of any accounting system. Financial accounting, representing as it does a reporting of current financial conditions and results of overall operations, must have as its base as accurate as possible a reporting of the actual or historical costs. The use of standards does not involve the elimination of actual or historical costs; rather in its most complete application it involves the presentation of historical costs in two parts, separating from the part which is standard the part which represents a variation from standard. Thus, the recording of actual historical costs in the form of totals is not abandoned, for

---

[1] Actual cost is used here to mean the cost which is accumulated during the process of production by the usual historical costing methods as opposed to the cost which has been determined in advance of the production process. The term "actual" is not intended to convey any implications as to the accuracy with which costs are measured.

[2] "The Uses and Classifications of Costs," *N. A. C. A. Bulletin,* Sec. II, May 15, 1946 p. 939.

they are still essential in determining the financial results of operations and as a check upon the standard costs.

By the same token historical costs alone are not enough. If a business is to be managed and controlled some advance indication of costs is essential. For cost control, planning, and pricing, management needs predetermined costs. Whether these predetermined costs are merely mental guesses made by the persons involved, formal estimates which can be used later for comparison with actual costs, or complete standards which are incorporated into the books of account, there is general agreement with the idea that some predetermination is desirable if not essential to successful business management. Any disagreement is likely to relate to the degree of coordination of predetermined costs with actual costs, rather than to the need for them. This can readily be seen in an examination of the historical development of the application of standard cost accounting.

## HISTORICAL DEVELOPMENT OF STANDARD COSTS

Estimates of cost were employed for pricing and for costing inventories before there was any formal cost accounting. However, early cost accounting was almost entirely historical in nature. Process or job-order methods were used to compile actual costs. The men who designed these cost systems had often been trained in the financial accounting field and they developed their cost accounting plans primarily to supply the inventory and cost of sales figures which were needed for the preparation of financial statements and product costs for use in pricing. At this time the most usual approach to improvement in cost accounting was thought to be through provision of costs in greater detail by the wider application and betterment of job-order cost recording.

### Influence of the Scientific Management Movement

With the scientific management movement came the development of industrial standards for use both in planning manufacturing operations and in evaluating the effectiveness with which work was being done. Perhaps the best definition of such an industrial standard is the following:

"A standard under modern scientific management is simply a carefully thought out method of performing a function, or carefully drawn specification covering an implement or some article of stores or of product. . . . The standard method of doing anything is simply the best method that can be devised at the time the standard is drawn." [3]

Such standards were a great improvement in the basic data used by management for two reasons, viz.:

1. They were based upon systematic observation, measurement, and controlled experiment—all factors which meant a marked increase in reliability.

2. They were recorded and made generally available within the company.

[3] Morris L. Cooke, quoted in the *Cost and Production Handbook*, p. 304. This definition has been adopted by Webster's Unabridged Dictionary.

These early standards were, of course, engineering or physical standards expressed in methods of operation, units of material, and hours of labor. The fundamental standards used to plan and control production in the factory are still of the same type. However, it was soon discovered that the same approach could be used in the control of manufacturing costs. This process developed in two directions:

1. Translation of physical standards into unit cost standards to be used in accounting for direct material and direct labor costs.

2. Development of budgets as a basis for controlling indirect costs which were not controllable by unit cost standards.

Historically, standard costs as we now know them and business budgeting developed at about the same time but in the earlier years their development was largely separate. Standard costs developed in the factory while budgeting was applied first to the financial aspect of business. Later on it was realized that both were merely applications of the same management philosophy and that they were complementary parts of a complete program of cost control.

### Standard Costs vs. Estimated Costs

It seems that the direct antecedents of modern standard cost accounting methods were estimating costing methods. Examples of the early use of such costing plans are common in the manufacturing of textiles, shoes, and fabricated brass products. Cost accounting methods used by these businesses commonly relied upon estimates prepared in advance for detailed product unit costs. The estimated unit costs were sometimes incorporated into the books and used to cost factory production. Estimated costs were then compared in total with actual costs and, if the differences were materially significant, inventory and cost-of-sales figures were corrected to reflect approximate actual costs.

However, these estimated costs were not standard costs. The distinction between them has been brought out by one writer as follows:

"A great difference exists between modern standard costs and the cost estimates maintained by some mills, which they sometimes confuse with standard cost methods. Approved predetermined costs reflect what the cost of each style should be and represent the results expected from the mill. Actual results are carefully controlled and kept within the standards in all possible cases. . . . Thus while standard costs are considered as representing the real cost with the actual results accordingly gauged, estimated costs are merely guesses with periodic attempts to reconcile them with actual operating results. Older cost methods . . . merely look to the operating results. Modern standard cost accounting methods decide what the costs should be and then take steps to realize these standards through actual operating." [4]

With the development of standard costs, the technique of incorporating predetermined costs into the accounts was utilized for costing production, with the

---

[4] Clinton W. Bennett, "Some Phases of Woolen Mill Cost Accounting," *N. A. C. A. Year Book*, 1922, pp. 341-342.

standard costs replacing estimated costs. Some accountants then began to use standard costs rather than actual costs for inventory costing on the theory that the planned costs provided a better basis for stating the cost of products remaining in the closing inventory than did the actual costs. However, this point of view was not accepted by all who used standard costs.

One writer has summarized this difference of opinion as follows:

"Accountants, generally, appear to be divided into two groups over the question and their views are almost diametrically opposed. One group holds that costs can only be "actual" costs, and that, therefore, standards, no matter how useful from a statistical standpoint, should not be reflected in the general records. This group, however, will modify their beliefs to the extent of permitting the elimination from costs of variances due to idle plant capacity, but they feel that all other forms of variances are merely fictitious debits and credits which should be ignored in the general records. Another major group of accountants holds that standard costs are "true costs" and that any excess over standard costs is a waste, and, therefore, a proper profit and loss charge. Their contention is not so much that this excess over standard is not a *cost,* but that it is a *cost of waste or inefficiency* and should not be confused with *cost of goods or product.* " [5]

In the course of this development operating executives found that it was more profitable to concentrate attention upon the deviations of actual from standard, rather than upon the actual costs. Hence, instead of merely using the variances to convert predetermined costs to an actual basis, the variances are now reported in terms of personal responsibility for cost incurrence and used by management in its efforts to control costs.

### Development of Standard Overhead Rates

The development of predetermined overhead rates which took place in the early years of the present century also contributed heavily to the line of thinking which has crystallized in the present-day concept of standard costs. It was realized that actual unit costs which could not be determined until the end of the period, and which fluctuated with the volume of work done in the factory because of the fixed cost component were not satisfactory costs either for inventory costing or for pricing purposes. Accordingly accountants began to use predetermined rates for applying or absorbing indirect costs. These rates were designed to obtain full absorption of fixed costs at a normal rate of activity and to exclude the costs of maintaining idle facilities from the costs of producing goods. When predetermined overhead rates were adopted, reported unit costs no longer increased when volume declined and decreased when volume increased. As a result accounting costs were made more useful. With the refinement of methods for

---

[5] Clifford G. Wood, "Disposition of Variances from Standard," *N. A. C. A. Bulletin,* Jan. 1, 1939, p. 548.

setting overhead rates, these early predetermined rates became the standard overhead rates of present-day cost systems.

While standard overhead rates successfully met objections to actual overhead rates for the purposes of costing production and for pricing, they had comparatively little value in the control of costs. The principal reason for this is that indirect costs are made up of expenses which differ widely in their controllability. The over- or underabsorbed overhead as determined by the earlier cost systems reflected the combined effects of variations from standard volume and variations in the amount spent. The next step was to devise ways for measuring performance in spending apart from the variations in cost due to fluctuations in activity. This required that standards be set to show how much indirect costs should be for any given rate of activity in the plant. Until this was accomplished, control of indirect costs was much less effective than the control exercised over direct costs.

Development of indirect cost standards which management could use to obtain better control of this element of cost required, first, that cost standards be set in terms of the expense allowable for the actual volume of production rather than for the normal volume used for cost absorption, and second, that the classification of costs used for cost control purposes be developed in such a manner that costs, both actual and standard, would be listed according to persons in the organization who possessed authority to incur each specific item of cost. This offered little difficulty with direct costs, but with indirect costs the problem was considerably more complicated.

The first indirect cost budgets were of the fixed type based upon the production forecast for the period ahead. Thus the expense allowance provided for the period was that considered proper for the volume of activity which was anticipated in the forecast for the period. However, these budgeted amounts of expense were suitable control standards only when the actual level of activity happened to be the same as that forecast when the budget was prepared. While this difficulty could be overcome to some extent by shortening the budget period and by revising the factory budget when the actual volume of activity differed from that forecast, these methods seldom achieved satisfactory results.

This shortcoming of the fixed budget was overcome by the development of the flexible or variable budget which provided operating management with an indirect cost standard for any level of activity which was likely to be met. Flexible budget standards accomplished this aim by being designed in the form of a schedule from which could be read the amount of expense which should be incurred at any given level of activity within the range of the budget. Variances from the budget standard could then be interpreted as the result of spending more or less than the standard figure for the actual volume of work done during the period.

Thus it is seen that the trend of cost accounting over the years has been toward broadening its usefulness. It began as a bookkeeping technique used principally for building up the inventory and cost of sales figures needed for the financial statements. As such it was almost entirely historical in character. While management has always needed to know what future costs are likely to be for the purposes of planning production and setting prices, it formerly could obtain this data only from estimates which were often not related to the costs recorded on the books.

With the development of standard costs, cost accounting became a valuable tool which management could use to control direct costs. This control was later extended to indirect costs through the development of flexible budgets. The improved reliability of costs based upon a set of good physical standards together with the forward-looking character of standard costs has also greatly extended the usefulness of cost accounting as a source of data that management can use to advantage for planning and pricing. In this process, the standard costs have merely replaced the estimates and unscientific opinions which were formerly used for purposes where predetermined costs were needed. Whereas these predetermined costs were formerly kept apart from the books, it is now common to incorporate the standard costs into the accounting records. In doing so, the cost accountant has usually simplified his work and has broadened its usefulness to management.

### Differences of Opinion Regarding Uses of Standard Costs

At the first Annual Conference of the National Association of Cost Accountants, held in 1920, there was a session entitled "The Relation of Cost Accounting to Business Management." While the papers which were read at this session and the discussion which followed showed that there was a lively interest in standard costs at that time, they also disclosed the existence of wide differences of opinion with regard to the uses and applications of standard costs. Many of these same questions have been raised at practically every discussion of the subject in the years which have followed. Some of these differences are largely differences of terminology. Thus standard costs have also been called scheduled costs, specification costs, predicted costs, planned costs, predetermined costs, and budgeted costs. While the terms employed have been the basis for many debates, they are not matters of great importance today. Other differences represent genuine divisions of opinion with respect to the nature and purposes of standard costs. It is these differences which are the subject of this inquiry.

It appears that many of the controversies over standard costs have their root in the different uses which are made of cost figures. In "The Uses and Classifications of Costs" it was stated that "Many of the apparent differences of opinion among cost accountants are not fundamental but arise from failure to recognize that cost data prepared for one purpose may not be appropriate for other purposes." [6] This statement applies to standard costs as well as to actual costs. In the preceding pages it has been shown that standard costs are not an alternative to actual costs but that rather the choice lies between standard costs and the less scientific cost estimates. The remainder of the study is devoted to a consideration

---

[6] *N. A. C. A. Bulletin,* Sec. II, May 15, 1946, p. 939.

of the applications of standard costs to meet the needs of management for costs to be used for the purposes of cost control, inventory costing, budgetary planning, and pricing.

## Standard Costs for Cost Control

### How Costs Are Controlled

Cost control has as its objective production of the required quality at the lowest cost attainable under existing conditions. It presupposes a plan or program which is embodied in a set of standards specifying how each job is to be done and what it ought to cost to do it. Operation under the standards then proceeds by comparing actual costs with the standard costs as the work is being done and by taking appropriate action to correct unfavorable deviations from the standard costs as such deviations occur.

However, cost control is not exclusively or even primarily an accounting process, although accounting methods do have an important part in cost control. In general, operation control must precede cost control. The problems of developing product specifications, operation methods, and operation times are a responsibility of the engineering or operating division of the business; hence, the control standards which are based upon production methods are established by the production division. On the other hand, it is the duty of the accounting department to measure performance relative to these standards and to keep management informed as to the effectiveness of its efforts in cost control. The matter of how best to bring the costs under control is then again an operating rather than an accounting function.

### Type of Standards Most Useful for Cost Control

Standards which are to be applied for cost control must provide answers to the following three questions:

1. For what should costs be incurred?      3. Who is responsible for control of the costs?
2. How much should the cost be?

These topics will be discussed in the order listed above.

### For What Should Costs Be Incurred?

Standards should be set for each cost item of consequence. Product unit costs are built up from their components since the cost of a finished product unit is made up of materials, labor, and overhead. Each of these cost elements ordinarily represents various quantities of different materials, a number of separate labor operations, and a more or less extensive variety of manufacturing facilities and services. Effective control requires detailed standards to show how much of each material should be used, how much labor should be required for each operation, and what facilities and services will be needed. The actual number of separate standards required to give this detail will be governed by the complexity of the manufacturing process, but in all cases the standards should tell exactly what should be used to accomplish the task.

Such control at the factory operation level is primarily a matter of controlling quantities and usage of material, labor, and services. Hence for the foremen and other employees who are directly in contact with the work it may be preferable to state both standards and variances in terms of physical units—i.e., in pounds of material, hours of labor, etc. However, when details are combined in summary form for the use of supervisory employees, it then becomes necessary to state standards as dollar costs. The actual quantities consumed are likewise priced at standard rates in order to permit measurement of cost performance under quantity standards free from the influence of price changes.

### How Much Should the Cost Be?

In order that a standard may specify how much should be spent to accomplish a given task, it is necessary to determine, first, the "tightness" with which the standard is to be set, and second, how the total amount spent will change with the level of activity in the cost center.

The tightness with which standards are set differs widely among users of standard costs. In this respect, standards vary from those which are well above possible attainment down to those which are merely averages of uncontrolled past performance. While these standards merge into one another and cannot always be clearly separated in practice, the following standards may be distinguished here for purposes of discussion.

1. *The theoretical, ideal, or perfection standard.* Such costs represent the best performance possible with the equipment in the plant. Some allowances for rest periods and personal needs of operators will probably be included in the standard, but no allowances for waste, spoilage, or lost time are made when setting the standards. It is not expected that such standards will be attained in actual operations, but the standards are set up as goals toward which to work in the attempt to improve efficiency.

2. *The attainable good performance standard.* This standard does not eliminate all waste, spoilage, lost time, etc., but includes these elements to the extent that management considers them impractical of elimination during the time the standard is to be in effect. A standard of this type can be met or even bettered, but only by what is regarded as efficient performance.

3. *Average past performance standard.* Standards are sometimes based upon what has been done in the past without adjustment to reflect methods which may be subject to improvement and without elimination of past wastes and inefficiencies. Since jobs on which performance is poor are likely to be more numerous and more extreme than are jobs on which performance is exceptionally good, such a standard is usually considerably looser than are standards of the preceding types.

Where the standards are too tight, there is no definite and known objective which employees can reasonably be expected to meet. They soon realize that the goals set for them are unattainable and cease to pay serious attention to the standards. Management finds it difficult to hold employees responsible for variances when it is not known what portion of the variance represents avoidable inefficiency and what portion represents cost reduction which could be obtained by perfection. Concerning a standard of this type William M. Lybrand has remarked that ". . . there will always be opportunity to explain away or excuse the failure to reach it." [7]

While it is sometimes said that an unattainably tight standard provides an incentive to reduce costs, it seems that this use of the standard confuses the objectives of cost reduction and cost control. Cost reduction proceeds by finding ways to achieve a given result through improved design, better methods, new layouts, incentive plans, etc. Hence cost reduction results in the establishment of new standards. On the other hand, cost control is a process of maintaining performance at as near existing standards as is possible. If standards are tighter than performance currently attainable, the lower cost will not necessarily follow unless the cost reduction program has first shown a practical method whereby the tighter standard can be attained. On the other hand, a standard which is set so loose that it can be met by poor performance buries the very inefficiencies that standard costs are intended to disclose.

Thus it would seem that the type of standard most effective in the control of costs is one which represents an attainable level of good performance. Such standards provide definite goals which employees can usually be expected to reach and they also appear to be fair bases from which to measure deviations for which employees are held responsible. A standard set at a level which is high yet still attainable with reasonably diligent effort and attention to the correct methods of doing the job may also be effective for stimulating efficiency.

It is not possible to define more precisely the exact level at which to set a control standard, for it is a question of judgment applied to the specific circumstances. It is also a matter which will change from time to time, for standards which were difficult to meet in the beginning may be too low at a later date when the methods underlying them have become familiar to the employees.

In determining how much should be spent, consideration must also be given to variations in cost which accompany fluctuations in the level of activity. The effect which volume fluctuations have on cost is easily handled when the costs are direct costs, since here the total amount which should be spent varies proportionately with the number of units produced. Direct costs can be satisfactorily controlled by unit cost standards. On the other hand, indirect costs cannot be controlled with standards in unit form because the average overhead per unit tends to vary as the volume of production increases or decreases. This, of course, results from the presence of costs which do not vary with production volume.

To meet this difficulty the cost standards used to control variable indirect cost are set in the form of a flexible budget which gives the total amount of each cost which should be incurred at each level of activity within a specified range. By comparing the actual expense with the standard amount shown by the flexible budget for the actual rate of activity, it is then possible to obtain a variance which reflects the effectiveness of operating performance.

[7] "Relation of Cost Accounting to Business Management—From the Viewpoint of the Professional Accountant." *N. A. C. A. Year Book,* 1920, p. 66.

### *Material and Labor Price Standards*

Ordinarily material and labor price standards have a comparatively limited value in exercising control over costs. However, material price standards make it possible to measure certain aspects of purchasing performance. Thus increases in material costs which result from purchase in uneconomical lots or from failure to take advantage of lowest cost transportation can be brought out as material price variances. Controllable labor price variances may also arise from the use of men with the wrong rate for the job. Even though operating management cannot control prices, the development of price variances may be useful in keeping top executives informed regarding the effect which changes in these cost influences will have on profits. Price standards are also necessary in order to permit measurement of cost performances under quantity standards, for otherwise it is not possible to say what portion of a variance is due to a deviation from the quantity standard and what portion has resulted from a change in price.

To the extent that price standards are used for cost control purposes, it seems that these standards need to be attainable and current and in this respect the problems of setting them are similar to the problems encountered in setting quantity standards to be used for cost control.

### *Who Is Responsible for the Control of Costs?*

Because costs must be controlled by individuals it is essential to have both standard and actual costs classified so that individual performance in cost control can be measured. As stated by C. H. Eckelkamp:

> "Cost centers should be established and divided into as many units as are deemed necessary to assure proper control, clearer presentation of data, and placing of individual responsibility. . . . It is axiomatic that responsibility for operating the budgets should be fixed as near as possible to the point of action and placed upon the individual who is charged with the responsibility of the operation and the attendant expenses." [8]

This requires a plan of cost classification which follows the organization structure in order that the costs which each individual can control may be assigned to him. Experience shows that this control is most effective when standards are set in terms of personal responsibility for each cost incurred and actual results are then measured against the respective standards in order that each individual may know how his performance compared with that which was expected of him.

For the purpose of measuring efficiency, only those costs which are direct with respect to a specific function need to be taken into consideration. Many costs which must be allocated in order to determine product costs can be treated as direct charges for purposes of control. For example, if a company produces its own electricity the head of the power plant is responsible for the cost per kilowatt hour. The cost of fuel used to produce power is thus a direct responsibility

---

[8] "An Approach to Budgetary Control," *N. A. C. A. Bulletin,* June 15, 1947, p. 1261.

of the power plant engineer. The other departments determine the amount of power needed and hence are responsible for the number of kilowatt hours used, but they do not control the cost of fuel consumed in the power plant.

Inclusion of allocated costs in statements prepared primarily for cost control purposes is avoided by some companies in order that departmental executives need review only those costs for which they are held directly responsible. Other companies do show allocated costs in control statements because they consider it desirable to have the departmental executives know the cost of facilities which they use. However, these companies usually separate allocated costs from directly controllable costs in the statements furnished departmental executives.

While cost classification on the basis of controllability is sometimes confused with the classification of costs as fixed or variable, it is a different problem. All costs are controllable by someone in the organization at some time. Costs like depreciation and property taxes are ordinarily considered to be fixed costs, but they are controllable at the management level where decisions to purchase, rent, or dispose of the related assets are made. Hence all costs should appear at some place on some control statements and costs which the departmental executives cannot control are the responsibility of top executives such as the plant super-intendent or company officers.

Moreover, control of costs is a matter of timing as well as placing of responsibility. Since any effect which standard costs can have in controlling costs must come before or at the time the costs are incurred, the standards must be applied to the source of the costs. As stated by Verne Breitenbucher:

"Cost control is concerned with charges at the point of origin. It is inseparably bound to the physical action or condition that generates the charge. Cost must be controlled and consequently reduced at the point where it is incurred." [9]

The exact point at which control may be exercised most effectively depends to a certain extent upon the circumstances in each specific case. Thus in controlling material costs, the price and quality may be best controlled at the time of purchase while control over the quantity consumed must be deferred until the materials are used.

When standards are applied at the source, actual operation costs may be matched with corresponding standard cost and any variance reported to the person responsible as soon as possible. Thus it is not uncommon to find daily reports of labor time, material usage, and other readily controllable costs. The alternative, which is to price production reports and ascertain variances at the end of a month or longer period, provides much weaker control since composite variances are difficult to analyze and the variances will have had a chance to accumulate before the condition is known. However, this method may be expedient for material price and other variances over which day-to-day control is not

---

[9] "Putting Cost Accounting to Work—For Cost Control," *N. A. C. A. Year Book,* 1946, p. 99.

generally attempted. Costs of long-lived assets can be controlled only when the assets are acquired, but control over the utilization of such assets calls for frequent reports of variances from the normal percentage of operation.

### Revision of Control Standards

Control standards must be kept up to date if they are to be accurate measures of the efficiency with which work is being performed. Hence revision seems essential when important changes take place in methods of production, labor efficiency, or material specifications. Changes in price have no effect upon the control of operating efficiency in the plant and it may be unnecessary to revise price standards at the same time. However, to the extent that price standards are used to measure purchasing efficiency or the matching of workers' man rates to the job rates to which they are assigned, price standards must also represent current conditions.

The amount of expense and effort involved in revising standards is quite large when many individual standards are in use. However, changes in the standards for particular components of cost need not always require a complete change all the way through to the finished product standard cost. Normally, general changes in labor rates, standard overhead rates, and substantial engineering changes dictate the desirability of completely revising the finished product cost through all of the ramifications of manufactured and purchased components, subassemblies, and major assemblies. However, changes involving only one component through material substitution, minor engineering specification changes, etc. can be accomplished rather simply from a clerical viewpoint by merely changing the standard for that particular component and by writing off variances between the two standards temporarily during the interim periods until a revised finished product cost standard is established. Through such a device, comparison between actual and revised standard performance is possible without the effort of a complete standard cost change.

### Standard Costs for the Control of Fixed Costs

While direct costs can be controlled with unit cost standards and indirect variable costs with flexible budget standards, the control of costs commonly classified as fixed requires standards of still another type. Control of these costs can be exercised in two ways, viz.:

1. By limiting expenditures to those called for by predetermined plans. Obviously this type of control is limited to the time before the expenditures have been made. However, much can be done to keep down fixed charges by carefully planning all additions to plant and by reviewing the need for personnel whose salaries make up part of the fixed charges. This planning will result in a fixed or appropriation type of budget which, in effect, be- comes the control standard for expenditures in the fixed charge group.

2. By securing proper utilization of the equipment and organization which the fixed charges represent. After machinery has been purchased or a decision made to maintain an organization of definite size, cost control becomes a matter of keeping these facilities employed at income producing tasks Hence

a standard of utilization is desirable in order that idleness of facilities may be brought to the attention of executives who may be able to prevent its continuance. The standard against which utilization of fixed plant and organization facilities is measured is the percentage of utilization of plant capacity set as normal.

For this purpose "normal" may be defined as a predetermined figure intended to remove from the overhead rate the fluctuations arising from seasonal, cyclical, and random influences. Another way of describing the normal standard is to say that it is set at a level which is expected to average out the ups and downs over a chosen period of time.

## STANDARD COSTS FOR INVENTORY COSTING

### Standard Cost vs. Actual Cost

While cost is generally recognized as the primary basis for the statement of inventories in the balance sheet, the historical introduction to this study has pointed out that some accountants use standard cost for inventory costing while others prefer to use actual costs. The difference lies in the concept of what constitutes cost for this purpose.

Thus one group maintains that a proper inventory cost is the planned or standard cost from which have been eliminated expenditures for avoidable waste or inefficiency and for the expense of maintaining idle production facilities.[10] These excess costs are viewed as period costs which should be charged directly against revenues rather than to inventory accounts. As expressed by one writer:

> "Generally, a more realistic profit determination will result if the ending inventory amount has been stated at a value no higher than the manufactured product costs which were planned and used as the base upon which the existing selling prices and policies were established." [11]

The other group maintains that inventory costs should include all costs incurred to manufacture the goods and that standard costs, if used for other purposes, should be adjusted to actual cost before the financial statements are prepared. The following quotation reflects this point of view:

> "Standards do not purport to be costs. . . . Their functions in the cost accounting system are to provide a convenient and flexible means of computing actual costs, inventories, and cost of sales, and to determine the extent of, and reasons for, variations of actual costs from expected results." [12]

The statement of inventories at standard cost will, of course, affect the period-by-period profit figures when a substantial portion of the actual cost is charged

---

[10] Discussions of this topic rarely mention variance gains, probably because they are, with the exception of volume variances, relatively unimportant in the aggregate.

[11] H. T. McAnly, "Should Unusual Costs Be Allocated to Period Rather than Product?" *The Journal of Accountancy*, May 1947, p. 432-33.

[12] Cyril F. Gamber, "The Relationship Between Standard and Actual Costs," *N. A. C. A. Bulletin*, April 1, 1946, p. 675.

against income of the current period through the closing of variance balances to cost of sales or other profit and loss accounts. This effect will be most marked when sales and production do not move closely together. However, revision of standard costs may cancel out the effect of writing off variances.

It may be noted that for the purpose of inventory costing, accounting for variances is primarily a matter of their proper disposal. The question of how or why they arose is important only when it affects the decision as to whether or not the variance is to be included in the figure used for inventory costing. This is exactly the opposite of the cost control problem, for there attention is centered upon the origin and cause of the variances while their ultimate disposal is not in question.

### Kind of Standard Most Useful for Inventory Costing

When the standard costs are to be used for costing inventories, the standards need to be current and reasonably attainable. When there is a substantial difference between standard and actual cost of the inventories, adjustment may be required unless there is definite justification for the difference. Thus in speaking of the use of standard costs in the postwar period one public accountant has said:

> "More frequent adjustments of standard costs must be made to meet our widely fluctuating operating conditions. The independent auditor must make sure that standard costs used for financial statements are soundly conceived and have been adjusted to represent current standards." [13]

Standards which are so tight as to be beyond currently obtainable performance cause large unfavorable variances to arise. When these are treated as period costs the inventories will not contain the full amount of manufacturing cost which is necessary for production of the goods represented by the inventory figures with the result that inventories are understated. On the other hand, a standard which is too loose will permit excess costs of waste, inefficiency, and idleness to be carried into the inventory.

A standard based on normal capacity would appear to be useful in costing the overhead element of cost in inventories because it tends to average out volume fluctuations. Where these volume fluctuations follow a fairly stable pattern so they can be predicted in advance, as do seasonal variations, a normal standard rate can be set which will accomplish this aim. However, the longer term cyclical fluctuations in volume often have no discernible periodic variation and substantial under- and overabsorbed balances may still arise.

It would seem that the same current standards based on attainable good performance are ordinarily suitable for both cost control and inventory costing, although many accountants will insist that for the latter purpose the standard

---

[13] J. Harold Stewart, "Developments in Cost Accounting During the War as They Affect the Auditor," in *New Developments in Accounting*, American Institute of Accountants, 1946, p. 49.

costs must not only be attainable but also attained by actual performance without large deviations.

### Application of Standard Costs for Inventory Costing

Ordinarily goods completed are charged to finished goods inventory account at the standard unit cost. This costing operation is performed as the goods are completed and transferred if a perpetual inventory account is kept, or at the time the physical inventory is taken if no perpetual inventory is kept. The credits to finished goods inventory and corresponding charges to cost of sales are likewise at standard cost.

Inventories of work in process at the end of the period are also costed at standard, although the time at which the standard costs are introduced into the accounts varies under different accounting plans. Thus, for example, debits to work in process account for material and labor may be for either the standard or the actual cost of these elements used, and debits for overhead may be for the standard cost of either standard or actual hours used. It is also common practice to charge work in process with the standard cost of some items and with the actual cost of other items. Thus variances may be separated at different points as the goods move through the factory. Any variances which have not been previously separated will appear when the work in process account is credited for the standard cost of goods finished or when the physical inventory is taken at the end of the period.

Raw materials may be carried at standard cost, the incoming materials usually being priced at standard cost and the price variance separated before the materials are charged to inventory. Under an alternative practice the materials inventory may be kept at actual cost and the price variance separated when materials are issued for use.

In actual practice it is found that partial applications of standard costs are rather frequently used for costing inventories. For example, inventories may contain actual cost of materials and standard cost of labor and overhead.

Variances developed through the application of standard costs for inventory costing are usually totals only since the more detailed information used for day-by-day cost control is commonly obtained directly by summary of the requisitions, scrap tickets, operation time cards, etc. Thus in a discussion of the subject, Harry E. Howell has said:

> "It would seem that the variance accounts recorded on the books would not be set up so as to draw off shop control reports because that would already have been done at the source. Instead the accounts should be set up to facilitate more accurate disposal of the variances, to disclose the effect of them in the financial statements, and to prepare long-term trend reports for top management guidance." [14]

---

[14] *Contemporary Accounting,* Thomas W. Leland, ed., American Institute of Accountants, 1945, Chapter 17, p. 7.

### Revision of Standard Costs for Inventory Costing

It has been stated above that standard costs for inventory valuation need to be current standards in order that inventories may reflect price and efficiency levels prevailing at the balance sheet date. Hence standard costs will need revision whenever cost-affecting changes of substantial amount take place. The following statement illustrates this point of view:

> "If a company does not change its standards very often I think it would be very sound to reflect in this year-end inventory valuation some adjustments indicating the variance between actual experience during the year and the standards set up. However, if you change your standards frequently as we do in our company (we change them once a year), and the new standards really reflect the economies that have transpired during the year, then we believe that no further adjustment is needed in the new standards since they already reflect cost reductions or cost increases, as the case may be." [15]

When standard costs are not revised often enough to represent current price and usage rates, it will likely be necessary to adjust inventories from standard cost to approximate actual cost. The standard costs thus serve as a starting point from which to compute actual costs by the use of ratios reflecting the differences between actual and standard cost of material, labor, and overhead. When it is desired to state inventories at actual cost, the use of standard costs in such a manner may still facilitate the bookkeeping processes by eliminating a certain amount of detailed tracing of costs.

## STANDARD COSTS FOR BUDGETARY PLANNING

### Relationship Between Standard Costs and Budgets

It has already been pointed out that budgets and standard costs are similar in that both are based upon the idea of predetermining the results and using comparison of actual performance with planned performance to measure progress toward the predetermined goal. When standard costs are used the budget is largely a summary of standards for all items of income and expense.

### The Place of Standard Costs in Budgeting

The budgetary plan is expressed in a forecast profit and loss statement and costs are needed in the development of this statement. In considering the cost side of the budget, it is necessary to determine the volume of production and sales and the probable cost of the things needed to produce the volume of goods called for in the budget.

Standard costs are especially valuable for this purpose because they provide a reliable and convenient source of data for converting the budgeted production

---

[15] Thomas H. Patterson, *N. A. C. A. Year Book*, 1941, p. 117.

schedule into requirements for raw material, labor, and services. The reliability of standard costs stems from the fact that they have been based upon careful studies of material usage requirements, operation methods and times, variability of cost with volume, and the best arrangement of equipment. Furthermore the standards have been tested and performance under them has been recorded so there is a good basis for predicting what performance can be expected in the future. On the other hand, past actual costs used alone usually reflect many temporary or random influences so that it is difficult to predict the future behavior of unstandardized costs.

Standard costs are more convenient than actual costs for budget preparation because the standard costs of operations and products are readily built up into total costs for any volume and mixture of products called for by the budget. When actual costs are used for such purposes a great deal of analysis and adjustment will usually be required. This is likely to be true particularly when the budget calls for extensive changes in product volume or product mixture.

### *The Use of Standards for Budgeting*

The costs to be used for budgeting should reflect:

1. The prices which are expected to prevail during the budget period for material, labor, and services.
2. The efficiencies which can be expected in the use of material, the application of labor, and the utilization of facilities and services.
3. The influence of volume or rate of activity on costs.

It is, however, well known that when standard costs are used for cost control and for inventory costing, variances will arise because actual costs cannot be kept exactly in line with standard costs. Hence in preparing the budget it will generally be necessary to forecast the variances which may arise during the forthcoming budget period. The amounts of the several variances thus anticipated will depend upon the specific standards used in preparing the budget. Where both standards and budget are based upon an assumption of attainable performance and where the standards are current, these variances are likely to be relatively small. On the other hand, if operating standards are very tight, if standard costs do not reflect current price levels, or if the volume of production will differ considerably from normal, then it is important to estimate the variances in order that the budget may give a realistic picture of expected operations.

Thus, when the standard costs do not provide exactly the costs needed for budgeting purposes, the forecast of variances provides a means whereby the standards can be utilized in preparing the budget without losing sight of the difference between standard costs and cost actually expected in the budget period.

### STANDARD COSTS FOR PRICING

Pricing is a matter of choosing the most advantageous course from among a range of possible alternatives. Furthermore, selling price and cost are each cause and effect of the other. The selling price per unit affects the number of units that can be sold and the resulting volume affects both the cost and the investment in production facilities. Hence it is necessary to select the best combinations of price, volume, and product mix and the selection may differ according to the length of time it is to remain in effect.

## Advantages of Standard Costs for Pricing

Standard costs are ordinarily more easily adjusted and projected into the future than are past actual costs for the following reasons:

1. Standard costs are based upon carefully determined usages of material and labor and thus are free from accidental distortions caused by excess spoilage, reoperations, etc. To the extent that these latter items are avoidable by competitors, they are probably not recoverable in selling price.

2. Adjustments to make standard costs reflect changes in material prices or labor rates are easily made. These adjustments can be made at any time, while standard costs entered on the books and used for inventory costing and for cost control can remain unchanged until the end of the year.

3. Standard overhead rates are based upon a normal activity level and thus provide an acceptable basis for prices which will provide for full recovery of overhead costs in the long run. Actual unit overhead cost at any given time may be so influenced by temporary volume fluctuations as to make actual cost entirely unusable for pricing. For short period pricing decisions the flexible budget standards provide data regarding variability of overhead with volume of activity. From these standards it is possible to secure an estimate of marginal costs which cannot be had by using historical data.

4. For pricing purposes, management needs to know the complete cost of manufacturing and marketing its products. Relatively few companies find it practical to assign marketing costs to products by regular bookkeeping methods, but standard costs can be set for marketing activities.

Factory costs for pricing must be in terms of product units rather than in terms of operations and in this respect pricing standards are more like standards for inventory costing than standards for cost control. While the determination of product unit standard costs for inventory costing sometimes raises difficult problems of applying indirect and joint factory costs to products, these problems are likely to be even more serious in the development of pricing standards. The reason for this is that an arbitrary division of joint costs can be quite satisfactory for inventory costing but not usable for price decisions. When such difficulties are encountered, complete product unit costs may not be obtainable and management must think in terms of securing the return of these joint costs in total out of the margin between aggregate sales revenues and the sum of all product costs.

## Standard Costs for Long-Run Pricing

The objective of long period price policy is to set prices on the company's products which will return all expenses of carrying on the business plus a reasonable return to the owners. The principal problems in developing such costs are centered around the method of recovering fixed costs in the selling prices of individual products. Unit cost standards which reflect fixed cost at normal volume will be the most useful for the purpose. By use of such standards, a cost is obtained which spreads the fixed costs evenly over the units of product made during a relatively long period with the result that the short-term variations in average unit cost are smoothed out. While short-run considerations may require deviations from prices based on long-run cost, the long period cost figure does serve as a guide which indicates the average prices which must be secured over a period of years in order to recover the company's investment in durable assets and continuing expenses for maintaining an organization ready to produce goods.

### Standard Costs for Short-Run Pricing

When attention is shifted from long to short period pricing, the variable costs of production then become more significant than the fixed costs. The objective of short-run price policy must be to cover the variable costs and to obtain, in addition, as large a contribution to fixed costs and profits as market conditions at the time will allow. This usually means that there will be periods when prices return all costs and yield a substantial profit besides and also periods of depression when the company must accept prices on some products which return something less than all fixed costs.

For such problems in pricing it is necessary to have the clearest possible separation of fixed and variable costs in order that management may know how much costs will be increased by accepting a given order, or how much cost can be saved by declining the order. The flexible budget standards will be especially useful here because from them can be obtained an estimate of the variation in overhead cost which can be expected to accompany changes in volume of production.

Again it appears essential that standards be up to date and representative of current material prices, current labor rates, and attainable performance efficiency. As stated by George C. Lyon:

"Where the cost department has the heavy responsibility for making prices, or for furnishing information on which prices are made, it is of the utmost importance that the standards used are not only correctly derived but that they reflect a practical goal rather than the ideal performance. . . . It makes a rather unfavorable impression on management to contend that certain standards must be attained because time study and engineered standards prove they can be made, when the actual results in terms of profit or loss demonstrate plainly that the ideal standards have never been attained and that a price based on those standards does not produce a profit." [16]

When standard costs are below actual current costs, prices may be set which fail to return the full outlay necessary to produce goods to fill the orders. On the other hand, standards which allow inclusion of avoidable waste in cost or which do not reflect realized cost reductions may handicap the sales department in securing its share of the market.

---

[16] "A Standard Cost Application in the Textile Industry," *N. A. C. A. Bulletin*, Aug. 1, 1946, p. 1140.

As all of the costs must be recovered out of the sales revenues, the costs required for pricing will not be limited to the costs included in inventories. For example, the costs of selling and general administration are part of the total cost but are not usually included in inventories. There may also be manufacturing costs which are not charged to inventories but included in costs used to guide the pricing of products. An example of this latter class of costs might be depreciation on assets which have been fully depreciated but which are still serviceable and in use.

## STANDARD COSTS TO FACILITATE BOOKKEEPING

### How Standard Costs Can Save Clerical Expense

The use of standard costs can often save clerical expense by eliminating the detailed record keeping which is necessary when actual costs are used alone. The principal points at which standard costs can be applied to reduce clerical expense may be listed as follows:

1. By carrying inventories at standard cost, stock ledgers can be kept in terms of quantities only. This eliminates much clerical effort in pricing and balancing items on stock ledger cards. Total standard cost of goods on hand can readily be obtained at any time by multiplying the quantity in stock by the standard unit cost. If average actual cost is wanted, it can be computed by multiplying standard cost by the ratio between actual and standard cost of the goods.

2. When standard costs are used, requisitions or bills of material for materials to be put into production can be written and priced more rapidly than when the goods must be priced at actual cost.

3. The standard cost of goods finished can be obtained immediately upon completion since it is necessary only to multiply the quantity by the unit standard cost. Simple and eco-nomical process costing methods can be used in place of elaborate job costing methods.

4. The time required to prepare reports which are used by management can be reduced. Since most reports are useful in proportion to their timeliness, the managerial value of accounting is considerably enhanced.

5. The time which must be devoted by management to study and interpretation of cost reports is much reduced when standard costs are used. These economies result from elimination of all details except those requiring attention and from the provision of standard figures which facilitate comparison and interpretation of actual costs.

6. The time required to assemble cost data for budget preparation or pricing studies is reduced because it is not necessary to devote so much time to the analysis and rearrangement of past actual costs.

### Application of Standard Costs in Record Keeping

The stability of the standards is of particular importance for record keeping economy, for changes in standards require time-consuming adjustments. When the application of standard costs is limited to those uses which produce economies in record keeping, the level at which the standard costs are set is relatively unimportant.

If the advantages of saving pricing calculations and the related postings in materials stock ledgers are to be secured, the standards must be applied upon entry of the materials in inventory records. On the other hand, if standard costs are to be used only to facilitate costing of finished goods inventories, the standards need not be applied until credits are entered in the work in process account.

### RECONCILIATION OF CONFLICTS IN DEVELOPMENT AND APPLICATION OF STANDARD COSTS FOR DIFFERENT PURPOSES

*The Problem of Conflicts*

In outlining the problems involved in developing and applying standard costs for each of the various uses of cost data, it will be noted that different types of standard costs were found to be needed for different purposes. Furthermore, in practice the standard costs are applied at different points in the bookkeeping process and handled in different ways.

It is obviously impractical to have different sets of standard costs for each purpose. Hence the remainder of this study is devoted to a discussion of possible ways of reconciling the conflicts.

*Differences in Application of Standard Costs*

Some firms incorporate standard costs into their accounts whereas others maintain them only for statistical comparisons without their incorporation into the double-entry system of cost records. When not incorporated, the standard costs may be used for the purposes of cost control, pricing, and budgeting, but they are not ordinarily used for inventory costing. Moreover, the advantages flowing from the saving of clerical effort in bookkeeping cannot be obtained, although cost control reports can still be constructed according to the principle of exceptions.

Even when the standard costs are entered on the books the standards may be applied at various points in the accounting cycle. The two principal points are (1) when the costs are incurred—i.e., at the time charges are made to work in process account or to records which are subsidiary to this account, and (2) when goods are completed—i.e., at the time work in process account is credited with finished production. An additional variation occurs with materials, for here the price standard may also be applied when the materials are charged to raw materials inventory account.

By the first method listed above, the standards are applied at the source of the cost. Variances are here developed currently as the operations take place and in detail. By the second method, the standards are applied in costing completed work. Variances are usually in the form of a total by orders, processes, or periods. While they may be obtainable by elements of cost, they usually must be analyzed before they can be traced by causes, departments, or operations. For this reason, the method is less effective for cost control than is the first method which permits development of variances by operations as the work progresses.

### Conflicts in Kind of Standards Used

The consideration of conflicts between different kinds of standard costs may be approached by considering first the purposes which usually cause standards to be incorporated into the accounts, since the modification of standard costs to serve varying purposes is most difficult when the standards are tied into the system of accounts. These purposes are the control of costs and the costing of inventories. Standard costs need not be entered on the books when used solely for budgeting or pricing.

For both inventory costing and the control of costs, the need is for current standards at an attainable level of efficient production insofar as direct costs are concerned. Hence the same standards can usually serve both purposes. With respect to overhead, the control standards are found in the flexible budget while the inventory costing standard is the normal overhead rate since cost control requires controllable cost at actual volume of activity and inventory costing calls for total overhead at normal capacity volume. However, these are related if the normal rate is derived by dividing the units of production at normal into the total overhead budgeted for this level of activity. Under these circumstances there would again seem to be no problem. With the same set of standard costs acceptable for both of these purposes, cost control reports can be drawn directly from the books and the same standard costs can be used for inventory costing.

When the standard costs in effect for cost control purposes are considered unsatisfactory for inventory costing, the problem can often be resolved by devising a variance disposal procedure which yields inventory costs of the desired type. As one writer has remarked, ". . . the inventory may be adjusted at any time to reflect those elements of cost fluctuations which created the variance. The problem is no different than that created in an actual cost system by a sudden drop in market prices, in which event inventories carried on the books at so-called actual cost must be adjusted to the lower of cost or market by the application of write-downs or reserves." [17]

In general, the first use made of variances is to keep management informed regarding performance efficiency. Their use for this purpose is not affected by the disposal made of the variances in the accounts. Thus some companies prefer not to use standard costs at all in their financial statements and therefore divide the variances between inventories and cost of sales in order to state inventories at approximate actual cost. Others use actual price combined with standard quantities and standard burden. With any of these methods of variance disposal, the variances can still be used for cost control purposes and the advantages of using standard costs in the books to facilitate the bookkeeping process can be retained while at the same time approximate actual costs are available for stating inventories on the balance sheet.

---

[17] Cyril F. Gamber, "The Relationship Between Standard and Actual Costs," *N. A. C. A. Bulletin*, April 1, 1946, p. 677.

While it would seem that the same standard costs can be used equally well for both inventory costing and cost control, problems may develop in the practical operation of a standard cost system. For example, price standards may have little or no control value and hence they may not be revised as often as necessary to provide satisfactory inventory costs. Or, a large volume variation gain may raise doubts concerning the desirability of crediting the entire variance to income when substantial inventories of manufactured goods are on hand. When such conditions occur, consideration should first be given to the desirability of revising the standards. If standard costs are revised, the year-end inventories can then be shown at the new standards. So long as a set of standard costs is to serve two purposes, both purposes must be kept in mind continuously in deciding when revisions should be made. On the other hand, revision of standard costs requires adjustment of the records and tends to reduce the bookkeeping economies derived from standard costs. Hence, the frequency with which standards entered on the books are revised must be a compromise between the need for keeping the standards current and the expense required to set new standards and to adjust the records.

Another problem may arise in connection with overhead costs. Since a number of overhead costs which are commonly included in inventories are not controllable within the comparatively short periods for which operating budgets are generally prepared, the content of the control budget is likely to differ somewhat from that of the budget used to develop overhead rates for inventory costing. Thus prorated fixed charges and variable costs which are not controllable by operating personnel may be omitted from the budgets used for cost control purposes but included in the standard overhead rate used to cost production. In other instances costs such as major repairs which occur irregularly are placed in the control budget of the period in which the work is done, while for inventory costing purposes the same costs are spread over the periods which benefit but in which no expenditures are made.

Cost control requires application of standard costs as closely as possible to the point of origin of the costs to be controlled. For good control it will therefore be desirable to apply the standard to each operation and to obtain and report the variances at frequent intervals. For inventory costing, the standard costs are not needed until manufacturing costs for the period are summarized. The same is true for pricing purposes where only total product costs are needed. However, application of standard costs at the source does not stand in the way of subsequent use of the same standard costs for other purposes since the standard operation costs can be summarized by products for inventory costing purposes.

If the standard costs are to be used for inventory costing but not in a program of detailed operation cost control, maximum advantage from the standpoint of bookkeeping simplification may be secured by deferring application of the standards until the inventories are costed. A combination of methods is sometimes found advantageous. Thus one company applies its material standards at the end of the production process and obtains a total material cost variance which is analyzed only occasionally. On the other hand, actual labor costs are compared with standards at the source and daily variance reports are prepared. The reason underlying this combination of methods is that material is a relatively unimportant portion of the total product cost at this particular company so the standard cost is applied to material principally for costing. Labor is the principal element in product cost, with the result that standard costs are applied in detail to control labor costs.

The use of standards for cost control may advantageously be applied to marketing and administration activities as well as to manufacturing. Since marketing and administration costs are not included in inventories, these standards are not used for inventory costing purposes.

The necessity for converting material usage, labor, and machine time standards into cost standards is sometimes questioned. The following statement represents this point of view:

"... if we control the time and material we control the cost ... if we control the time and quantity we can be contented to allow the cost to be whatever it may." [18]

On the other hand, there are advantages to be gained by converting physical standards into cost standards and entering these on the books.

These advantages are:

1. Where the relative importance of variances is not known in terms of cost, expensive time may be wasted to save cheap materials or vice versa. Or much effort may be applied to reducing variances that represent insignificant costs when more important ones are neglected.

2. Executives above the shop foreman level must use summarized data to keep informed. Cost furnishes a basis upon which all operations can be reduced to comparable terms and summarized in reports that are understandable even by those who are not familiar with the detailed operations underlying them.

3. Physical standards have no usefulness for such purposes as inventory costing and pricing, but cost standards are distinctly useful for these other purposes as well as for cost control.

4. Physical standards cannot be used to study the gross profit by classes of products, customers, or marketing operations.

This is not to say that physical standards should not be used where they are superior to cost standards for the purpose. Possibly the use of cost standards has even been carried too far in their application for cost control at the shop foreman's level. Thus one writer has said that:

"The most effective plans for cost control are those which are direct and simple and which permit performance to be measured on the spot by a visual check....

"Types of budgets which provide visual control are those expressed in terms of physical units. ... This is true whether the cost system is operated on the basis of the various types of standard costs or on an actual cost basis. In most instances, however, physical standards are converted into dollar values, and control in the shop is effected on a financial basis. On the other

---

[18] Arthur Lazarus, "Standard Costs," *The Journal of Accountancy*, April, 1923, p. 251.

hand, there are some organizations that do use the standards or estimates which are established in physical terms for the purpose of factory cost control. This latter method is, of course, the most direct and should be the most effective for shop control purposes." [19]

Standard costs which are to be used only for budget preparation or for pricing need not be entered on the books. However, standards for budgeting and pricing are not entirely unrelated to the book standards, but are commonly derived from the latter by making appropriate allowances. When it is desired to retain the present book standard costs for inventory costing and cost control, the effect of the allowances can be shown in the budget by including a forecast of variances.

On the other hand, it may be considered best to revise the book standards to reflect the changes anticipated. In this event new standard costs will be prepared and entered on the books. Thus the same standards used in preparing the budget will also be used for costing inventories and for cost control and a forecast of variances need not be made.

Standards for short-run pricing need to be kept in line with current material prices, wage rates, and labor efficiency since most companies prefer to base their prices on costs which they actually expect to incur. Long-run standards should be revised when changes in methods or equipment bring permanent alterations in cost. In industries where goods are made on a special order basis, it is necessary to estimate costs for pricing each job according to the specifications of the product. The book standards will supply standard data which can readily be adjusted as desired without conflicting with the use of standards incorporated into the books for other purposes.

For all purposes, the usefulness of standard costs will be much influenced by the care with which they have been set and maintained. Many instances of failure to use them and of management's expression of a desire for actual costs rather than standard costs reflects a lack of confidence in the standards. If they are known to be merely guesses, to be set at an unrealistic level, or out of date, management may justifiably question their reliability and doubt the wisdom of spending money on them.

---

[19] David B. Caminez, "Controlling Costs with Physical Unit Budgets," *N. A. C. A. Year Book*, 1944, pp. 148-49.

# Chapter 2

## STANDARDS TO AID CONTROL OF MANUFACTURING COSTS

COSTS of production are affected by internal factors over which management has a large degree of control and also by external factors over which management has only limited control. One of the first steps in the development of a plan for cost control is the separation, as far as possible, of noncontrollable factors from those factors which are controllable. In this respect standards are valuable aids. Since the scope of managerial control over material usage, labor performance, and overhead spending is more direct than it is over prices paid and production volume, the main emphasis of this paper will be on standards for the cost factors first named.

Control over costs is best effected through action at the source. Hence the standards used need to be specifications for the quantities of material, labor, and services to be consumed in performing an operation rather than the complete product cost standards. Variances from these standards should be developed to show causes and responsibilities for deviations from standards. Corrective action to eliminate variance causes lies in the field of management, but operating management relies on the accountant for facts which make possible intelligent executive action toward control of costs.

### MATERIAL QUANTITY STANDARDS

Material quantity standards are based upon the standard bill of materials which, in turn, is developed from the product specifications. The material quantity standards thus tell what kind and what quantity of material should be used to make the product desired. These physical quantity standards are the primary basis for material cost control; they are converted to cost standards by multiplying the standard quantities by unit material price standards for the purpose of measuring material cost variance.

### Setting Material Quantity Standards

There are three methods in use to set material quantity standards. These may be described as follows:

1. Engineering studies to determine the best kind of material for the purpose and the proper quantity to use. This requires a consideration of the production methods to be used, quality of the product to be made, expected yield, and similar factors.

2. Analysis of past experience in usage of materials for the same or similar products. In setting standards by this method past performance is averaged or the standards are based on jobs or periods which are selected as typical. The use of unadjusted past ex-

26

perience may include in the standards an un-determined amount of past waste and excess usage. Known excess usage may be elimi-nated in setting the standards or the stand-ards may be tightened by an arbitrary per-centage reduction in the quantity of material allowed, but the method does not focus at-tention on finding the best combination of quantity, methods, and product quality as does the engineering study method. However, the use of past experience may be less costly and quite satisfactory in setting standards for minor items of cost or perhaps for obtaining temporary standards.[1]

3. Test runs under controlled conditions. This method avoids some of the principal short-comings of the preceding method in that conditions can be standardized and extrane-ous causes of variation eliminated. Most com-panies use a combination of the above methods in setting their material quantity standards, although approximately two-thirds of the companies interviewed reported that they rely principally on engineering studies.

### *Allowances Incorporated in Material Quantity Standards*

When material quantity standards are set by engineering study, the calcula-tion of standard quantities from drawings and product specifications yields theo-retical or ideal quantity standards to which allowances must be added to get the attainable standards needed for control. While the allowances that are made de-pend partly upon the nature of the production processes, nearly all of the com-panies interviewed increase the quantities of material included in the standards to cover a certain amount of wastage and loss that is considered impossible or impracticable of elimination. Thus in metal working there are turnings, chips, and butt ends cut off; in chemical processes losses occur by leakage, evaporation, etc. A company manufacturing asphalt roofing states its procedure for setting standard material quantities as follows:

> "The laboratory determines what materials and quantities will be needed to make the product wanted. This is an ideal standard. Following this a processing loss allowance based on experience is added to get the standard usage. Included in the allowance are such items as leakage of asphalt, evap-oration losses, damaged ends of felt rolls, trimmings, etc."

In addition to the above, approximately half of the companies include an allow-ance in the standard quantity to cover direct materials spoiled in processing.

Material losses in manufacturing may be kept apart from rather than included in the material quantity standards.[2] A separate cost standard is then established for such losses. In some cases this is treated as a separate cost item, but usually it is included in the overhead budget.

---

[1] As stated in the accounting manual of one company, "The ultimate effectiveness of pro-cedures will be determined by ability to set good performance standards. Where such stand-ards cannot be set with a high degree of accuracy at the outset, much can still be accom-plished by setting approximate standards. . . . The variances resulting from measurement of actual expenditures to standard may not be 100% controllable, but by segregating them in such a way that they can be analyzed, it will be possible to obtain factual data upon which to base more accurate standards in the future and thereby set up a more effective control of manufacturing costs."

[2] For example, the standard cost manual of a manufacturer of electrical equipment states that: "Our product costs are set up on the basis of using exact quantities per unit as pre-scribed in the bill of materials. Since exact quantities cannot be adhered to, even under the best of manufacturing operations, a standard spoilage allowance is provided for in the standard product cost sheet."

### Tightness of Quantity Standards

Approximately two-thirds of the companies interviewed reported that their material quantity variance accounts occasionally show favorable balances at the end of a month whereas the other one-third stated that their net material quantity variance is seldom or never favorable. While the absence of favorable variances may be an indication of tight standards, favorable variances may arise from changes in factors not completely controlled or allowed for in the standards. Thus several companies reported that they could not change their standards as often as changes occur in production methods or product specifications and hence favorable quantity variances occur when these changes reduce the quantity of material actually used below that allowed by the standards. In addition, conditions which affect yield from materials cannot always be entirely controlled and standards are set for average performance thus making favorable variances possible. Examples here are the effect of humidity on textiles or the lack of uniformity in raw materials like leather or cork.

On the other hand, favorable variances may occur because standards are loose and easily exceeded by performance. It is interesting to note that in six cases it was stated that occurrence of favorable variances was viewed as an indication that standards had been set too loosely.

### Effect of Conditions of Supply

Setting of material standards and the use of these standards for cost control is made difficult when conditions of material supply make it necessary to use substitutes or to accept materials which do not meet standard specifications. Scrap losses, reoperations, and rejected product are thus likely to be large and difficult to predict. Setting the standards loose enough to cover all of these items tends to weaken the control value of the standards, while tight standards result in large variances for which operating personnel cannot be considered responsible. The prevailing opinion seems to be that the best procedure is to maintain tight control standards and then to make an analysis of variances as to cause, with such extra allowances or separation of noncontrollable items as is possible before assessing responsibility on operating personnel.

### Frequency of Revision

Since material quantity standards are based on product specifications and production methods it might be expected that changes in the standards would accompany changes in these specifications. This expectation is borne out by the field study, for four-fifths of the companies interviewed revise the material quantity standards used for current cost control whenever changes in methods or products affect the kinds or quantities of material used. The remaining companies review material quantity standards periodically and make any changes which may be necessary at that time. Most of these companies review their standards annually.

Regardless of the infrequency with which standards for costing inventories are revised, it would seem necessary to make changes in standards used for cost control whenever there are definite changes in product specifications affecting material usage, if good cost control is to be maintained. It is evident that some of the companies which change their material standards infrequently make little use of these standards for cost control purposes.

### Responsibility for Setting Material Quantity Standards

Material quantity standards are usually set by the department which is responsible for product design and for operation methods in the factory. While specific titles vary, the engineering department was mentioned most frequently as setting material quantity standards. Five of the companies interviewed have separate standards departments although some of these are under engineering supervision. In the smaller companies where a separate organization unit for the purpose of setting standards is not needed, the task of setting material quantity standards is usually delegated to an individual familiar with products and manufacturing methods.

It is common for more than one department to participate in setting material quantity standards and the production and cost departments are often mentioned as assisting. This makes it possible to utilize the knowledge and experience possessed by these departments and also helps to obtain their cooperation in making the standards effective. The production department itself rarely sets material standards since it is considered undesirable for the persons held responsible for meeting the standards to have final authority to set the standards. While the engineering department is usually a part of the production division of the business, it reports at a sufficiently high level to give it the independence needed in setting standards.

In the field study several companies reported that material quantity standards are set by their cost departments. In some of these cases the material cost standards are used primarily for bookkeeping convenience and not for cost control purposes.

### Application of Material Quantity Standards for Cost Control

Control of material costs is aided when each person possessing authority to use material knows in advance exactly what quantity of material he should use to obtain the desired quantity of product. Furthermore, he needs to know how successful he is in meeting the standard and it is desirable to have these facts reported to him and to those who supervise his work. These reports will be most effective if made in time for adjustments or corrections to be made before any unfavorable tendencies can accumulate into large losses.

In the factory, this means placing detailed quantity standards for each operation or process in the hands of the foremen and reporting variances to them. Production executives with supervisory authority over the foremen are more concerned with over-all results than with details, but they should also receive variance reports. Through these variance reports they are kept informed regarding performance of the foremen in controlling costs and thus they can better judge when they should take action to correct unsatisfactory conditions.

The specific procedure for matching actual usage with the corresponding standards is influenced by a number of factors, among which the following appear to be most significant:

1. The nature and value of the materials.
2. The type of accounting plan used.
3. The methods used for detecting and measuring losses of material in production.
4. The extent to which cost reports are employed by management for purposes of cost control.

These factors will be discussed in the order listed above.

1. *The nature and value of the materials.* Usage of some materials can be predetermined quite exactly and actual usage accurately accounted for. Purchased parts such as electric motors or valuable materials like gold are examples. On the other hand, usage of materials such as lumber, coal, or scrap iron is not accurately controlled because of the nature of the material or its low unit value. Usage standards for these materials represent average consumption and variances are collected as totals for a period of time.

2. *The type of accounting plan used.* Where a job order production plan is in use, the material variance is usually determined for each order. If a process plan is in use, the material usage variances are determined periodically.

3. *The methods used for detecting and measuring material losses in production.* When the production order calls for a definite quantity of product and an underrun is not permissible, the actual quantity of material used can be compared directly with the standard quantity specified in the bill of material. A requisition or bill of materials is prepared for the standard quantity of material needed to make the number of product units called for by the production order. The workmen are thus provided with the standard quantity of materials for the job. If additional material is needed to complete the quantity of product called for by the order, excess quantity requisitions are prepared. These call attention of factory personnel to failures to meet the standard. Variance reports for executives having supervisory authority over production are prepared by periodic summaries of the excess quantity requisitions.

When the quantity to be produced is not definitely fixed, it is necessary to consider the amount of good product that should have been obtained from the actual quantity of material used. This procedure may be reversed by determining how much material should have been used for the quantity of product obtained. Variances are the result of excess scrap or substandard yield from processing resulting in less than the quantity of product called for by the order. Pricing recorded production at unit standard cost for material gives the standard material cost. The material quantity variance may be determined by comparing this figure with the standard cost of the actual quantity of materials used. Where the product is put through in lots or orders the comparison may be made at the completion of each order; where production is on a continuous process basis, comparisons are made periodically.[3] In the latter case it is necessary also to consider any materials in the work in process inventory.

A weakness of this method is that the variance is not available until some time after the losses have occurred. If details are wanted as to the causes of the variances and responsibility for them, it is necessary to analyze the variance totals and to trace them back to their sources. At this time it may be too late to stop specific losses, although action can still be taken to keep them from continuing. For this reason methods are often used for detecting and measuring the more important material losses at a point nearer their source. The following are typical procedures:

   a. The work is inspected at designated points in the process of manufacturing. Reports of rejected work are prepared and losses of material resulting from rejections are charged to a variance account.
   b. Scrap and spoiled work put aside by operators is measured and cost of any such material loss in excess of standard is charged to a variance account.
   c. Yield of good pieces from each process or operation is compared with the standard yield from the amount of material used. Shortage or overage tickets are prepared and used as the basis for determining the material quantity variance.

There will usually be residual material quantity variances not detected by the above methods. However, they will be disclosed when the work in process account is cleared of the standard cost of the work. Variances which are too small to justify separate measurement can be picked up in this way.[4]

4. *The extent to which cost reports are employed by management for purposes of cost control.* Some companies rely upon physical quantity standards for detailed control of material usage, and variances in terms of cost are developed only at the end of the accounting period, usually in connection with an annual physical inventory.[5] From the control point of view, the cost variances serve principally as an over-all or summary measure of how effective the physical control has been during the year.

---

[3] Thus a machinery manufacturer reports that in its foundry the pig iron usage variance is determined as follows: "Each shipment of pig iron is put into inventory at standard price. Daily reports of the material charged into the cupola form the basis for a monthly adjustment between actual pig iron used and the standard amount which is based upon the output of net good castings."

[4] A woolen mill charges the soaps, dyes, and chemicals used in scouring and stock dyeing to work in process inventories at standard cost. Variances due to usage of these materials are then determined by the differences between book inventory figures and the physical count when the semi-annual physical inventory is taken. The cost represented by such variances is relatively insignificant.

[5] Thus a wire manufacturer states that its material quantity variances are small due to close physical control by the engineering department during the production process. The company therefore determines its material cost variance only at the end of the year when a complete physical inventory is taken. However, weekly physical usage reports are prepared for foremen.

Several companies interviewed enter only actual material cost on the books, but for control purposes they utilize standards in terms of quantities.

## Material Variance Analysis and Reporting

When variance reports are used for control of material cost the reports must provide adequate detail as to sources and causes of variances. They must also help to place responsibility for the variances.[6] The field study showed that such reports are prepared by summarizing material requisitions, scrap tickets, inspection reports, or other primary records rather than by drawing off variance reports from the books. This enables the reports to be made more promptly and avoids entry on the books of details that are not needed for costing production.

The field study disclosed that variance reports generally go to all those in the company management who are directly concerned with production. These include foremen, departmental supervisors, factory superintendent, vice president in charge of production, and in several instances the president. One company supplies reports to individual machine operators.

The field study showed that a number of companies maintained material usage control by the use of quantity standards and various on-the-spot checks which keep quantities close to prescribed usage. These companies often have such close control over material usage that they find it unnecessary to prepare detailed cost variance reports. In small companies, the closeness of management to factory operations also serves to keep executives informed concerning material usage, and variance reports are largely unnecessary.

## Follow-up of Material Quantity Variances

The use of standards is ineffective in controlling costs unless some systematic procedure is employed to make sure that action will be taken when important variances arise. Approximately half of the companies interviewed reported the use of regular follow-up procedures when material variances occur. These usually consist of a discussion of the variances at regular meetings of the executives concerned. At this time corrective actions may be planned, further investigations suggested, etc.[7]

Companies which reported no regular follow-up procedure to be in force were

---

[6] Analyses of material quantity variances are made regularly on the following basis by 33 companies interviewed in the field study.

|  | No. of companies |
|---|---|
| By type of material | 14 |
| By products | 10 |
| By job orders | 4 |
| By departments | 20 |
| By cause of variances | 16 |

[7] Other procedures reported by various companies are:
Persons directly responsible for a variance are required to report on cause and steps being taken to avoid recurrence of unfavorable condition.
Cost engineer spends full time investigating variances.
Supervisor makes an investigation and orders corrective action if he thinks it necessary.

asked what managerial action would be taken if a large material quantity variance should occur. In general, the answer was that the line executive having supervisory responsibility for costs would start an investigation and follow up the matter as far as he thought necessary.

## MATERIAL PRICE STANDARDS

### Usefulness of Price Standards in Control of Material Costs

As stated by the controller of one company visited in the field study, "Price variances are affected more by external conditions than by internal control."[8] Price standards make it possible to separate cost variances arising from excess usage and other controllable conditions from cost variances caused by changes in price paid for the materials and similar external conditions over which there may be little control. If the price standards had no other value in controlling costs it would seem necessary to have them for this purpose. However, price standards are used for measuring some aspects of purchasing performance and for measuring the over-all effects of price changes on costs and profits.

Material price standards usually represent what the actual cost of materials is expected to be instead of an efficient or desired price. Most of the companies interviewed in the field study reported that they base their material price standards on either a forecast of the actual price anticipated during the period that the standards will be in effect or on the actual price prevailing at the time the standards are set. The main problems which arise in setting material price standards relate to the use of standard costs for costing inventories and for pricing products. Hence, further discussion of how material price standards are set will be deferred to later chapters.

### Price Standards to Control Purchasing Performance

The purchasing department may exert some control over the cost of materials by buying in economical quantities, by taking advantage of the cheapest methods of transportation, or by approving invoices in time for payment during the discount period. Since most of the companies interviewed include freight inward in the standard material prices, it would seem that price variances arising from shipping by more expensive methods could be determined and responsibility therefor established. However, such a variance would not always be the fault of the purchasing department, for it could reflect failure of the factory to anticipate its needs, acceptance of a rush order by the sales department, or disturbance of transportation facilities by strikes, congestion, etc.

### Other Control Uses of Material Price Standards

Price standards are also useful in showing the effect that off-standard prices

---

[8] This was particularly true at the time this study was made. When an adequate supply of materials is available, management should have a larger degree of control over material prices in many industries.

will have on profits. Top executives are responsible for maintaining a proper balance between costs, selling prices, and volume of sales. In doing this the executive needs to be kept informed regarding the effect which changes in material prices will have on costs and profits, for action can sometimes be taken to counteract unfavorable effects that changes in material prices may have on profits. Thus substitute materials may be found which are less expensive, changes in product specifications or processing methods may be made, or selling prices may be increased. Initiation of such action is largely up to the top executives. For this reason the reports on material variances which indicate the need for such action are regarded as important control reports by many companies. This can be seen in the fact that in the field study it was found that reports of material price variances are generally supplied to top executives.

### Responsibility for Setting Material Price Standards

In the field study it was found that material price standards are usually set by the cost department, by the purchasing department, or by the two working together.[9] While the main task of setting material price standards is performed in these two departments, it was frequently stated that various other departments are consulted, give advice, or supply information. However, in many cases the process of setting a price standard is largely one of assembling relevant price figures since the standard is so often based on current market levels. The purchasing and cost departments are in possession of the data concerning prices and market conditions. Hence they prepare the forecasts or select the current price figures which determine the standards.

### Pricing Materials at Standard

In the field study it was found that three-fourths of the companies price materials at standard when the materials are received. The remaining companies apply the standard price at some subsequent point, usually at the time materials are issued. Companies in the latter group ordinarily make little attempt to use variances for control of material price since the variances are not known until some time after the materials have been purchased.

### Material Price Variance Reports

Most of the companies prepare monthly reports showing variances from price

---

[9] Following is a tabulation of replies received in the field study:

| Material price standards set by: | No. of companies |
| --- | --- |
| Purchasing department | 12 |
| Cost or accounting department | 24 |
| Cost department and purchasing departments together | 14 |
| Miscellaneous other departments | 12 |
| Total number of companies replying to question | 62 |

standards.[10] These reports usually go to top executives (president, vice-presidents, treasurer, and controller), to the purchasing department, and less frequently to the production department.

In a majority of the companies price variances are shown on a formal report. In some instances these reports are limited to a statement of price variances, but more often the price variances are listed along with the other manufacturing cost variances on a special variance report or on the statement of cost of goods manufactured. Reports confined to price variance information generally list materials classified by types of commodities and give the actual cost, the standard cost, and the variance for each class of material.[11]

Companies not showing price variances on a formal report bring significant variances to the attention of those concerned by such means as oral presentation, by having the persons responsible examine various records (e.g., invoices on which extensions at standard prices have been made, journal entries summarizing material costs, etc.), or by occasional preparation of memos. Usually these companies are small or purchases are few in number.

### Responsibility for Material Price Variances

To the extent that responsibility can be placed for material price variances, this responsibility generally is stated to rest with the purchasing department. From the interview reports it is quite evident, however, that the responsibility of the purchasing department for material price standards is more a matter of predicting what the materials are going to cost than it is for buying at the standard price. The attitude generally observed has been expressed by a writer on the subject as follows:

"These variances are not accepted, per se, as evidence that the purchasing department did a bad or good job of purchasing if the actual costs are greater or less than standard. It is taken as evidence of an error in fore-

---

[10] The tabulation below indicates the frequency with which these variances are reported by 62 companies which replied to the question.

|  | No. of companies |
| --- | --- |
| Quarterly | 3 |
| Monthly | 43 |
| Weekly | 2 |
| Irregularly | 2 |
|  | 50 |

The remaining 12 companies do not show price variances on any reports.

[11] A manufacturer of electrical equipment prepares three price variance reports showing different degrees of detail according to the needs of the executives who receive each report. In the first of these reports, supplied to general company executives, materials are grouped into a few broad classes to reduce details to a minimum. The second report, designed to keep accounting department executives informed, shows price variances classified by the inventory account code. The third report, prepared for those desiring details in connection with making price quotations, making up product specifications, etc., lists variances by specific materials purchased.

casting. There are many things affecting the prices of materials used in our business that are beyond the control of the purchasing department, and if too much criticism were made of a purchasing loss against standard, the natural reaction of the purchasing agent would be to make the next standards high enough to protect himself against any contingency. So we merely say to him that he is expected to make the estimate of standard costs as nearly on the nose as he can, and it has worked out to our advantage in eliminating inflated purchase standards from the profit forecasts."[12]

In a few cases it was stated that various top executives are considered responsible for price variances because they choose sources of supply and negotiate purchase contracts. On the other hand, approximately one-third of the companies interviewed said that they considered no one responsible for price variances.

### Follow-up of Material Price Variances

Very few of the companies interviewed reported that they have any regular follow-up procedure for price variances. The companies reporting no regular follow-up procedure were asked what action would be taken if large price variances should occur. The usual reply was that the variance would be the subject of a special investigation to ascertain the cause and to determine what action could be taken.[13]

### LABOR PERFORMANCE STANDARDS

One of the most fertile fields to which management can apply its efforts toward reduction and control of costs is the improvement of labor performance. A good set of operation time standards is well nigh indispensable for this purpose and the extension of these time standards into cost standards forms a logical completion of the labor cost control plan. The field studies showed that all of the 72 companies interviewed possess labor performance standards and that most of them utilize item and motion study methods to establish these standards.

### Setting Labor Performance Standards

The setting of labor performance standards is a process similar in approach to that employed for setting material quantity standards, but the techniques differ, as might be expected, where the problem is one of dealing with human operators rather than with inert substances. Establishment of standard operation times calls for determination of time needed to complete each operation when working under standard conditions. Hence along with operation timing goes the standard-

---

12 Thomas H. Patterson, *N. A. C. A. Bulletin,* April 1, 1945, p. 749.
13 Examples of typical comments concerning this procedure are:
　"The operating committee (composed of technical staff, sales, and production executives) discusses possible changes to reduce costs."
　"Operating officials talk it over with the purchasing agent to check possibilities of improvement."
　"We would consider the advisability of revising price standards."

ization of surrounding conditions that influence the effectiveness with which the employee performs his task.[14] The scope of such a standardization plan may be indicated as follows:[15]

1. Consideration of layout, condition of equipment, the workplace, and transportation facilities to standardize these and to provide the best practicable arrangement under existing circumstances.
2. Establishment of control over materials in order that the workman may have the correct quality and quantity available in the proper place. This will require investigation of purchasing, receiving, and storekeeping methods, of the plant transportation system, and the placing of materials at the workbench or machine.
3. Development of a system of planning, routing, and dispatching of work.
4. Provision of all needed instructions for the worker, either in the form of advance training or directions for each specific job.

The few companies that do not use time and motion study techniques for setting their labor performance standards obtain their standards by having the cost department study past performance or have the standards set by foremen who base them upon their experience, judgment, and knowledge of the operations. It appears likely that in such cases standards are used principally for costing production rather than for cost control. However, a textile mill has recently established standards by this method because it was thus possible to put a standard cost plan into operation within a short period of time. It has also instituted a program of time and motion studies through which it expects to effect a gradual tightening of standards as the studies of manufacturing operations disclose ways to improve present methods.

### Responsibility for Setting Labor Performance Standards

The setting of operation time standards requires an adequate technical background, for the standard setter must understand the processes used in the industry as well as the technique of time study. In addition, he should have sufficient independence to be impartial in establishing standards which serve as measures of individual efficiency and perhaps also as a basis for wage payment.

This combination of technical training and independence is usually obtained by delegating the setting of labor standards to staff specialists. Among the com-

---

[14] John W. Sheetz ("The Industrial Engineer, the Cost Accountant, and Labor Standards," *N. A. C. A. Bulletin*, Nov. 1, 1946, pp. 317-318) has thus emphasized the need for method studies in setting labor standards:

"The chief value of motion and time studies lies in the standardization of conditions and methods, the former representing the material things surrounding the operation and the latter the motions executed by the worker in performing the operation. Conditions and method in actual practice are inseparable. Almost every change of condition requires a change of method and many changes of method require changed conditions.

"Independent time studies without method studies have no permanent value. . . . This is so because of the improvements which are automatically made by the production organization. . . . Time study which has not effected any improvements in methods nor eliminated any waste of time or of labor will soon make the standard obsolete because of improvements in methods that normally occur. The method study is necessary for two reasons; first, to bring the standard costs down to a reasonably low level, and second, to insure a standard which is not only correct at the moment but which will remain so until some fundamental change has been made in the operating practice."

[15] See W. L. Walker, "Job Time Standards," *N. A. C. A. Year Book*, 1928, pp. 43-61.

panies using time and motion study methods, the usual practice is to have a department to set labor standards. This department has various designations among which are time study, industrial engineering, standards, rate setting, wage incentive, methods, and cost control. In small companies one or more time study specialists attached to the production or engineering department set the standards. In one case the standards were originally set by an outside consultant and subsequently revised by the company.

Companies not using time and motion study methods usually reported that labor performance standards are set by either the cost department or by foremen.

### Tightness of Labor Performance Standards

Time study men make allowances for fatigue, personal needs of operators, and unavoidable delays, in setting time standards. A little over half of the companies make no additional allowances in their labor cost standards. The remaining companies usually include additional time to cover work rejected by inspectors or "fall-downs" (usually failure to meet piece rate standard). In a few instances, other items such as allowances for machine set-up and change-over, machine breakdown, waiting time of operators, rework, and paid vacation time are included. However, most companies usually include the latter type of cost in the overhead budget instead of in the direct labor standards. This practice may be explained on the supposition that while these are includible in cost of production to the extent that they are unavoidable, they are not related to the efficiency of the individual operators. As such, they are best controlled through the overhead budget.

A number of companies stated that labor performance standards are, as a matter of policy, kept quite tight. Thus, one reported that its actual performance practically never exceeds 95 per cent of standard and usually ranges between 85 and 95 per cent of standard. These tight standards are designed primarily for cost control and where costing or pricing is the principal aim with control incidental, the labor standards tend to be looser.

Where favorable labor performance variances do occur, replies to questions with regard to causes of such variances indicated that most favorable labor performance variances arise from the following conditions:

1. Better than standard performance on day work since considerable fluctuation in output occurs when operators are paid by this method.
2. Labor-saving changes in methods, equipment, etc., which are not accompanied by concurrent changes in labor standards.
3. Mistakes in setting standards too loose.
4. Variations in performance which result when working conditions are not well standardized.

### Frequency of Review

Since operation time standards often serve as the basis for an incentive wage payment plan as well as for other purposes, the time standards, once set, are usually not changed until a change in method of performing the operation requires that a new standard be set. Most of the companies interviewed have their operation time standards under constant review and change individual standards when changes are made in the jobs to which the standards apply. Such changes are necessary to maintain the usefulness of the standards for cost control.

### Responsibility for Labor Performance Variances

Replies from the companies interviewed show that the foremen are almost always considered directly responsible for controllable labor variances and that production executives with supervisory authority over the foremen are held responsible for the foreman's success in controlling labor variances. However, foremen are not responsible for variances resulting from decisions which they did not have authority to make. For example, variances arising from such causes as the use of nonpreferred equipment are the responsibility of the departmental executive who directs the making of such changes.

### Labor Variance Pick-up

Since application of standards at the source of the cost provides the most effective cost control, frequent comparison of actual performance with the standards might be expected. The field studies show that this process of matching actual performance with the related standard is brought closer to the individual operation for labor than it is for the other elements of cost.[16]

While clerical procedures for reporting labor time vary, they usually make use of either a periodic report or a job time ticket. In either case the labor variance is commonly computed on these labor time records. The causes of such variances are usually noted on the original record through use of a code.[17] The causes of the variances are thus initially stated in terms which are familiar to plant management.

The field study disclosed a few companies which determine the labor cost variance only when a periodic physical inventory is taken. Most of these companies use time standards and calculate daily labor variances in hours for control pur-

---

[16] This can be seen in the following tabulation of variance analysis practice reported from the field interviews.

| Variances analyzed by | No. of companies |
|---|---|
| Responsibility (i.e. by departments, cost centers, or individuals) | 49 |
| Operations | 27 |
| Products | 15 |
| Causes | 28 |
| Job orders | 9 |

The total of the figures listed above exceeds the number of companies interviewed since most companies make analyses of labor variances on more than one basis.

[17] For example, a manufacturer of textile machinery uses a piecework labor variance report on which variance causes are recorded as follows:

114—Nonpreferred equipment or rerouted work
115—Breakdown
116—Idle equipment
117—Other piecework allowances
119—Hard castings

A copy of the above report is supplied to foremen at the end of each week.

poses. The labor cost standards are used only for costing inventories, but the control use of standards is actually well developed although not exercised in terms of dollar costs.

## Variance Reporting and Follow-up

Labor cost variances are usually brought to the attention of the individuals responsible for them by regular reports.[18] Reports prepared by companies interviewed generally contain other manufacturing cost variances in addition to the labor cost variance although daily or weekly reports going to foremen sometimes are limited to labor variances. These latter reports are ordinarily for departments or cost centers which coincide with individual responsibility for labor costs. Summaries of the departmental variances are also prepared to provide top management with the over-all picture of labor performance.

Approximately half of the companies interviewed have a regular follow-up procedure for labor variances while the remainder take follow-up action only when a large or unexplained variance occurs. Follow-up procedures observed are of the following general types.

1. The variances are discussed in a conference of executives interested. Causes and proposed remedies are brought up and corrective action may be recommended to line executives in charge of the operations producing the variances.

2. The staff department responsible for methods and standards investigates and determines what corrective action should be taken.

3. The responsible line executive investigates and institutes any changes that he thinks desirable.

4. Foremen responsible are required to report to their superior, explaining what caused the variances and what has been done or should be done to correct the situation.

The above are listed in the order of frequency with which they were mentioned in the field study.

## LABOR RATE STANDARDS

### Use of Labor Rate Standards to Control Costs

As with material prices, labor rates are determined largely by factors external to the individual company. Base rates paid are generally set by collective bargaining with unions or by the prevailing rate in the locality. Companies interviewed

---

[18] The frequency with which such reports are prepared by 62 of the companies replying to this question is shown below.

|  | No. of companies |
|---|---|
| Reporting variances monthly | 25 |
| Reporting variances weekly | 21 |
| Reporting variances daily | 7 |
|  | 53 |

Nine companies do not have regular reports of labor variances. These companies are mostly small and those individuals concerned with labor performance are kept informed by personal examination of original time records, by oral presentations of variances, or by memos calling attention to unusual situations.

stated that variances due to rate changes are usually unimportant in amount since it is general practice to revise the rate standards when actual base rates of pay are changed. However, rate standards are not without value in control of costs since some rate variances result from factors which are controllable by management.[19]

After a basic wage rate has been set, management exercises further control over what it costs to do a specific job in the plant through the design and administration of its wage payment plan. This comprises the use of job rating to establish proper differentials between rates paid for various jobs and the development of employee compensation plans which provide an incentive for the worker to give adequate production in return for the time he spends in the plant. These methods will, of course, influence the standard rate set for a specific job.[20]

### *Responsibility for Setting Labor Rate Standards*

The function of setting the labor rate standards is usually performed by the division of the business which has available the information from which standards are set. Thus in the field study the cost department was most frequently mentioned. Second in frequency was the engineering department (or a related division such as time study or standards), and in a few instances the rate standards are set by the personnel department.

### *Revision of Rate Standards*

Approximately half of the companies interviewed change rate standards whenever actual rates of pay change. An equally large group of companies reviews rate standards periodically, with annual revision being the usual practice. Two companies use long period normal rates.

It is thus apparent that most companies keep their labor rate standards closely in line with the actual rate being paid. Even those companies which reported periodic reviews frequently stated that the time of review corresponds with regular review of union contracts so changes in wage rates resulting from revision of the agreement with the union are immediately reflected in new labor rate standards.

---

[19] In the field study those companies developing labor rate variances were asked what caused rate variances to appear. The replies are tabulated below:

| *Cause of variances* | *No. of companies* |
|---|---|
| Variations from average rate used as standard, (due to overtime, learners, etc.) | 13 |
| Using man with wrong rate for job | 12 |
| Failure to have men on incentive | 5 |
| Rate changes, standards not revised | 7 |
| Variation in number of machines run per man | 3 |

It can be seen that management has control over some of these causes and that action could be taken to eliminate the related variances.

[20] As an illustration of practice in setting labor rate standards, one company has the engineering department specify on operation sheets the grade of labor to be used. The standard rate is then taken from a rate schedule prepared by the personnel department.

### Variance Analysis and Reporting

Only one-third of the companies interviewed develop rate variances and the use of rate variances for cost control obviously is limited. The lack of variance analysis supports this conclusion.[21]

Those companies developing rate variances were asked whom they consider responsible for rate variances and in half of the cases the foremen were mentioned as having at least some responsibility. These companies stated that the causes of rate variances which they experienced were usually using a man with the wrong rate for the job, failure of operators to earn piece rates resulting in payment on a more expensive day rate basis, or having too many men per machine.

While various ways of informing the foremen of rate variances were found, the usual method was to have the rate variances included on a regular report showing all types of variances for which the individual foreman is held responsible. However, other techniques are also used to direct the foreman's attention to jobs needing action.[22]

Only two of these companies reported any regular follow-up procedure for rate variances. One assigns a cost control engineer to investigate and the other takes up the variance in a conference between management and the accounting department.

The remaining companies developing rate variances did not mention the foremen as responsible for labor rate variances, but list various executives such as department supervisors, factory superintendent, manager of industrial relations, and president. These companies generally state that their rate variances arise from changes in wage rates without corresponding changes in the standards, variations from the average rate used as a standard, and similar causes. Variance reports are usually made monthly and go to the executives responsible or interested. Three companies report discussion of the variances at regular meetings of executives and in one company the manager of industrial relations is responsible for investigating the variances.

### Relationship Between Labor Standards and Incentive Wage Plans

Standards by themselves do not control labor costs, for in order to realize the costs predetermined by the setting of standards it is necessary that actual operation times be kept in line with the standard times. Experience has shown that one of the most effective ways of enlisting the cooperation and efforts of produc-

---

[21] Only 7 companies analyze rate variances by cause. However, 16 companies determine rate variances by departments or cost centers which, to some extent, localizes responsibility.

[22] Thus one small company sends job record tickets showing variances to the foremen daily and in another company the timekeeper supplies the foremen with a daily list of operations on which piece rate was not earned in order that the foreman may know which jobs need his attention. This company stated that it had found that its foremen are thus enabled to make better use of their time since they need not watch the operators in order to find out which jobs need attention.

tion personnel in meeting standards is to provide a financial incentive for doing so. This takes the form of employee compensation plans wherein the amount of wages paid is tied to performance under the standards. For direct labor where production of each employee is usually rather easily measured, various incentive wage plans are used which base wages earned upon production in terms of pieces, standard hours, or points.

Successful operation of these incentive wage plans requires reliable operation time standards. These standards are the same as those upon which the standard labor costs are based. Through such use of the same standards management can maintain its control over operation of the wage plan by using information provided by the cost reports. Thus so long as labor performance variances are small management can rest assured that employee productivity, earnings, and labor costs anticipated when the wage plan was adopted are being maintained.[23]

With indirect labor it is more difficult to develop an incentive wage plan primarily because standards are not so easily set for the tasks performed as they are for most direct labor. However, in some cases incentive payments are based upon cost performance of the employees supervised or upon performance measured by a budget.[24]

That the use of incentive wage plans is widespread among companies using standard costs may be seen in the fact that 60 of the 72 companies interviewed stated that incentive payment plans either predominate or are important in their plants. When a straight piecework plan of payment is in force the piece rate establishes the standard labor rate for the operation. Here labor variances will arise only when work is done on an hourly basis instead of the piece rate or when special allowances are made. These are usually made to protect the employee from some condition beyond his control, such as irregularities in quality of materials, machine trouble, presence of learners in the labor force, etc. Standard cost rates based on piece rates do not include items like vacation pay and wage increases expressed in cents per hour. It appears to be common practice to treat these payments as overhead costs rather than as direct labor.

## OVERHEAD COST STANDARDS

### Problems in Control of Overhead Costs

The general approach to control of overhead costs is basically no different from that applied to direct costs, for it proceeds by setting standards which are used to evaluate performance expressed in actual costs. However, the specific techniques of setting standards and the application of these standards differ in

---

[23] For an illustration of an incentive wage plan tied in with standard costs, see "Installing an Incentive Wage Plan," by Charles M. Reinherr and Paul Griek, *N. A. C. A. Bulletin,* Jan. 1, 1946, pp. 383-400.

[24] For an example of a bonus plan for salaried employees which is based upon standards, see C. L. Kingsbury, "An Incentive Bonus Plan Based on Cost Efficiency," *N. A. C. A. Bulletin,* May 1, 1941, pp. 965-978.

several respects from the techniques used with direct material and direct labor.

In the first place, overhead covers a complex variety of costs, the individual components of which behave in different ways when activity in the plant increases or decreases. Some overhead costs vary directly and proportionately with activity, others follow activity but not in the same ratio, and still others are largely independent of activity. As a result the actual average unit cost fluctuates with changes in activity and for this reason overhead standards for cost control are set in the form of budgets which give the total amount to be spent at a given level of activity.

Another result of the complex nature of overhead costs is that control over various items of overhead rests with different individuals in the organization. For example, foremen in productive departments may be able to control usage of indirect labor, superintendents may control factory clerical expenses, and heads of service departments control costs of supplying heat, cleaning, and plant transportation. Responsibility for costs must therefore be carefully defined.

The presence in overhead of costs which do not readily respond to changes in production volume requires a different approach to control.[25] Ordinarily control efforts must be directed toward obtaining the best possible utilization of the facilities to which the costs are directly related.

### Types of Overhead Cost Budgets Used

There are two types of budgets for controlling the variable component of overhead costs. These are the flexible budget, which provides allowances which vary with activity in the department concerned, and the fixed budget which provides an allowance for the specific activity level anticipated. When the flexible budget is used, it is generally expected that activity will fluctuate during the period the budget is in force and it is therefore necessary to have standards which show how expenses should change with volume. The fixed budget, on the contrary, is predicated on the expectation that activity will be at the level forecast and hence only one set of budget allowances is needed.

Approximately three-fourths of the companies interviewed in the field study were found to use a flexible budget while the remainder use a fixed type of budget.

An objection often made to the fixed budget is that control over expenses may be lost if the level of activity deviates materially from the level on which the

---

[25] As David B. Caminez has pointed out ("Budgets for Cost Control," *N. A. C. A. Bulletin,* Nov. 1, 1946, pp. 306-307), the manufacturing expense budget is really a consolidation of two separate budgets, i.e., a budget for fixed expenses and a budget for variable expenses. Usually the allowances in the fixed budget include the salaries and wages of supervisory and key personnel who would be retained on the payroll during a prolonged period of low-volume operations as during temporary shutdown conditions, the cost of fuel for heating, power demand charges, minimum maintenance to preserve buildings and equipment from deterioration, depreciation, property insurance, rentals, minimum telephone charges, etc. These things are fixed by managerial policy; an advantage of having them set up in detailed schedules is that they can then be reviewed and any desired changes made by management.

budget is based. The flexible budget was originally developed to overcome this objection. However, a number of companies reported that they are able to plan their production for a sufficiently long period in advance to avoid fluctuations in activity which would weaken the effectiveness of a fixed budget for cost control. This is perhaps to some extent a reflection of current market conditions which allowed steady production at practical capacity.[26]

### Setting Overhead Budgets

Usually the first step in determining overhead budget allowances is a study of past experience in the usage of indirect labor, supplies, and services.[27] Figures so obtained are then modified to reflect changes in wage rates, material prices, equipment in use, and ony other known influences which will make future overhead costs differ from those incurred in the past. Further adjustment is also commonly made by the exercise of managerial judgment. Thus allowances may be reduced or increased in comparison with past experience if management deems such action desirable.

Most companies budget overhead in dollars only. However, as with direct material and direct labor, overhead budget allowances may be based on determination of quantities (i.e. hours of labor, pounds of supply materials, kilowatt hours of electricity, etc.). The latter practice applies only to important items, minor items being stated as dollar allowances.

With overhead it is especially important that control be exercised at the source of the cost. After various prorations or distributions have been made the results of excess spending become diffused and it is virtually impossible to ascertain how much inefficiency has cost or who was responsible for it. The need for costing production generally leads to collection of overhead costs at specific cost centers. Up to this point, the accounting procedures can serve both the purposes of product costing and cost control, but after the costs directly controllable in the cost center have been distributed to other centers the figures lose their control value.

---

[26] Even where a flexible budget is in use, fixed budgets may be necessary for some departments in which costs do not bear a definite relationship to the volume of production. An example in point is the research department.

[27] The length of past experience upon which budgets are based by 24 companies is given below:

|  | No. of companies |
| --- | --- |
| Previous six months | 3 |
| Previous year | 10 |
| Two to five years | 8 |
| Ten years or more | 3 |
|  | 24 |

While the accounting period immediately preceding is most commonly the only one considered when revising budgets from year to year, a number of companies indicated that they studied a longer period of expense history at the time the first budget was prepared.

General recognition of this may be seen in the practice found in the field study.[28]

Departmental cost control budgets usually are limited to repetitive operating expenses and exclude such items as major repairs, construction work, and other irregularly occurring or unusual expenditures. These are provided for in the general budget and the work is controlled by estimates for each job done. However, a few companies do include an extra allowance in foremen's regular operating budgets for specific jobs which have been approved and over which the foremen have supervision.[29]

### Service Department Costs

The existence of service departments supplying services to productive departments raises a question of placing responsibility for costs of the various services. Approximately half of the companies interviewed charge these services to productive departments at standard rates which are based upon the expenses budgeted for the service department. The head of each service department is responsible for any controllable variances arising in his department. The budget of each productive department contains an allowance for the standard cost of the quantity of service which should be consumed. Hence, the productive department is responsible for the quantity of services used but not for the unit cost.

The remaining companies interviewed charge service department costs to productive departments at actual unit costs. Some of these companies hold the service department foremen responsible for service costs whereas some others consider the productive department foremen responsible. In a number of instances service department costs are not controlled with budgets or standards and actual costs are merely distributed to productive departments for costing products.

### Responsibility for Preparing Overhead Budgets

The accounting department usually prepares the overhead budgets. Since these budgets are based largely on past experience, the accounting department has apparently been chosen for the task because the principal source of historical cost data is contained in the accounting records. Furthermore, the accounting department possesses the technical qualifications for organizing and shaping into useful form the record of past experience on costs. It is not responsible for per-

---

[28] Somewhat over half of the companies interviewed include no prorated expenses in the budgets used for cost control purposes. The other companies do include prorated expenses in the control budget, but all pointed out that responsibility of the departmental executives ends with the expenses which they control and does not extend to the prorated items. In most cases the prorated expenses are included because the same statement is prepared for both cost control and product costing purposes, but a few companies indicated that they wished to tell the foreman the total cost of operating his department.

[29] Nonrepetitive maintenance and repair jobs such as overhauling motors and painting buildings are typical examples. One company has furnaces which are relined after two or three years of use. When this work is to be done, a special allowance for the work is placed in the control budget of that period. However, for production costing purposes, each period is charged with a portion of the cost.

formance under the budgets and hence has the independence needed to set fair standards.

Where the overhead budgets are not established by the accounting department, the task is usually assigned to a special department whose function it is to set standards.

In most of the companies interviewed executives of operating departments who are directly responsible for expenses aid in preparing their own budgets, approve the budgets before they are put into effect, or take both of these steps.[30] By this process their experience and knowledge of conditions is utilized in preparing the budgets and in addition better cooperation in use of the budgets as a tool for cost control results when the operating personnel participate in the process of standard setting. Several company executives commented to the effect that the budget conferences have a high value in making foremen conscious of the need for cost control.

### Revision of Overhead Control Budgets

Companies interviewed usually revise overhead control budgets annually, although a few companies make revisions semiannually or quarterly. While a number of companies revise their budgets only when they consider it necessary instead of at regular intervals, all of these companies using their overhead budgets for cost control purposes have revised them within the past year.[31] Thus it may be seen that overhead control budgets are current.

### Overhead Variances

It has been stated that budgets are prepared for each department or cost center and that these cost centers are the points at which control of overhead costs is exercised. The overhead variances developed for control purposes are obtained by comparing actual expenses with the standard expenses contained in the budget. This comparison is made for each item of expense controllable by the supervisor of the cost center. If desired, individual variances can be analyzed to determine specific causes, although this was usually found to be done only when significant variances occur.

The over-all overhead variances are reported in various ways. The field study showed that most companies develop a controllable variance and a volume variance. A few companies have three overhead variances, developing volume, spending, and efficiency variances.

Responsibility for meeting the budgets should be fixed as near as possible to

---

[30] A textile manufacturer thus reports that a committee made up of the operating executive in charge, the foreman of the department, and the cost accountant prepares the budgets.

[31] A textile company has described its method as follows: in the lower left-hand corner of the cost card there is a space for budget changes. Whenever operating conditions affecting costs have been changed by management since the standards and budget allowances were set, the budget allowance is properly adjusted. Such items as plant-wide increases, changes in manufacturing specifications, and introduction of new machinery are handled here. In this way the budget is always up to date.

48

the point where action can be taken to control expenses. Authority to control expenses and responsibility for them must be distinctly defined, for if there is óverlapping the budget will not operate satisfactorily.

Volume variances are rather commonly viewed as the result of outside circumstances over which the business has no control. While this may be true to a certain extent it would seem that it is the function of management at the over-all planning and policy-making level to secure a proper balance between production facilities and sales in order that losses from unutilized capacity may be kept at a minimum. For this reason some companies consider top management responsible for volume variances. Such control is necessarily a long-range problem and a volume variance in any given period may be something over which little direct control can be exercised.[32]

### Overhead Cost Control Reports

Reports generally show the budgeted expense, actual expense, and variance for the current period and cumulatively for the year to date. A report is prepared for each department or cost center listing items of expense incurred in the department and summary reports covering broader areas are prepared for executives above the rank of foreman. When the reports contain expenses which are not controllable by the person receiving the report, these expenses are often grouped together at the end.[33]

Most companies prepare reports on overhead budget variances monthly, although a few companies reported the use of weekly reports. The latter are sometimes limited to certain items of expense. Thus one company prepares weekly reports on indirect labor and also uses a monthly report covering all budgeted overhead expenses.

---

[32] A few companies reported exceptions to the above attitude toward volume variances. These are interesting in that they disclose a field where some immediate control over volume variances may be possible. Practice of these companies is summarized below.

*Company No. 1*—The sales manager is considered responsible for volume variances since he is expected to obtain the volume of business used in establishing the standard overhead rate.

*Company No. 2*—Departmental supervisors are held responsible for idleness due to machine breakdowns, failure to have materials or operators ready, and similar causes of delay in the factory.

*Company No. 3*—A manufacturer of office machines has a production stabilization program whereby the factory works at a steady rate and product is accumulated in inventory during seasonal periods of slack sales. The production planning department is held responsible for volume variances in production since such variances result from faulty planning of operations.

[33] As an illustration, the practice of a textile company is cited below.

A summary sheet shows variances for the entire plant by type of expense with a breakdown between variance due to volume and that due to controllable factors. This summary sheet is distributed to factory management, divisional management, controller's office, and to the vice president in charge of manufacturing. Detailed sheets are prepared for each department showing a comparison of actual expense with the budget adjusted for volume. These latter go to foremen and to factory management.

*Follow-up Procedures for Overhead Costs*

With only a few exceptions the companies covered in the field study have a regular follow-up procedure for variances from overhead budgets. The general method is the same as for material quantity and labor performance variances. Thus the procedures reported most frequently are discussion of variances at conferences, investigation by executives with line authority over foremen, and investigation by staff departments.

*Incentive Payment Plans Based on Budgets*

Only a few companies reported the use of incentive payment plans for foremen based upon the overhead budgets. Several companies expressed interest in eventual development of such incentive plans but do not have them in effect at the present time.

*Conclusions Regarding Use of Standards to Control Overhead Costs*

It is apparent that the control of overhead expenses is usually weaker than is control of direct costs. Thus many companies in which direct material and direct labor are closely controlled by standards have little in the way of overhead expense standards. Others do possess overhead budgets, but inquiry disclosed them to be used mostly for costing production. Furthermore, it seems that expenses of service departments are less effectively controlled than are the indirect expenses incurred in productive departments.

Doubtless this relative weakness of cost control stems in part at least from the difficulties involved in setting reliable standards for overhead costs. Where activities are varied and the individual items of cost are numerous and perhaps rather small, they are not as readily brought under control as are direct costs which arise from simple repetitive operations. Moreover, responsibility for the incurrence of overhead costs is not clearly defined in many organizations and control is therefore practically impossible to establish.

## CONCLUSION

*Factors Affecting Usefulness of Standard Costs for Cost Control*

Most of the companies interviewed regard usefulness in aiding cost control to be a major justification for employing standard costs. The effectiveness with which this aim is achieved varies. Based upon observations made in the course of the field study, the following conditions seem to accompany successful use of standard costs for controlling costs:

1. Management is interested in controlling costs, is aware of the advantages offered by standard costs for this purpose, and uses the variance reports.
2. Standards are reliable, current, and represent good but attainable performance. Management and operating personnel both have confidence in the correctness and fairness of the standards.
3. Reports are prepared which keep management at all levels informed of progress relative to standards.
4. The system of record keeping is as simple as possible.

On the other hand, conditions which appear to stand in the way of successful use of standard costs for cost control are:

1. Management is uninterested or unaware of the usefulness of standard costs. For this reason several companies having well-developed standard cost plans for product costing make little use of their standard costs for control purposes.
2. Standards are out of date, unreliable, or are designed to give product costs rather than operation costs. As a result of the first two conditions the standards are not taken seriously. The result of the latter condition is that variances cannot be traced to their sources without laborious investigation or are determined too late to be of much interest.
3. Reports are not prepared in terms which management understands. Executives with a production or sales background may not be able to interpret accounting terminology.

Several factors sometimes mentioned as determining the success with which standard costs can be used did not appear to be significant. These are:

1. The nature of the processes used or the products made. Companies were found using standard costs successfully in simple process type industries, in industries carrying on mass production of standard products of many types, and in job order industries where production was complicated and products built to special order. However, it was evident that the specific plan of using standard costs must be adapted to the needs of the company.
2. Size of the company. When a company is large enough to need records and reports to keep management in touch with operations, standard costs seem applicable.
3. Rapidly changing conditions of the postwar period. It seems that more frequent revision of standards is necessary, but effective use of standards was seen to be possible.
4. Cost of operating the standard cost plan. Most companies stated that they had obtained distinct economies in the operation of their cost systems through the use of standard costs. In some cases comments were made to the effect that introduction of standard costs required increased expenditures for engineering personnel needed in setting and maintaining standards. However, these companies were agreed that such additional expenses were more than offset by savings derived from improved control over production costs.

Numerous companies were encountered which were either revising and improving existing standard cost plans or introducing standard costs for the first time. These companies, together with those which had considerable experience with their standard costs, were, with few exceptions, agreed that standard costs provide management with a highly effective tool to aid in control of costs.

# *Chapter 3*

## STANDARD COSTS FOR COSTING INVENTORIES

STANDARD costs are usually placed on the books to facilitate the process of accounting for costs, particularly if standard costs are used for costing inventories. While standard costs need not be entered on the books in order to use them for purposes of cost control, pricing, or budgeting, incorporation of standard costs into the accounts probably strengthens the effectiveness with which standards can be used for purposes other than bookkeeping economy.[1] In the field study it was found that only four of the 72 companies whose methods were studied did not have standard costs entered on their books.

Bookkeeping can be simplified, clerical expense reduced, and reports prepared more promptly in many cases through the use of standard costs. The usefulness of the reports to internal management can also be increased, although this subject is more closely related to the use of standards for cost control.

### TYPES OF COST SYSTEMS

As the complexity of manufacturing processes increases and the number of products made in a plant grows, the problems which arise in determining product unit costs become more difficult. Likewise, the ascertainment of cost of goods in finished and in-process inventories becomes more troublesome. The development of accounting techniques to meet these problems has followed two somewhat different approaches. These are:

1. To use a job order cost system in which the manufacturing costs applicable to each order are recorded on a separate job cost sheet. The accumulated costs on the order cost sheets thus give product costs by orders and, by summation, provide the cost of the inventory. Job order costing is employed when it is desired to know the actual cost of in-dividual jobs and when separate accumulation of costs is not unduly expensive in relation to the value of the goods in the order.

2. To abandon the attempt to accumulate actual costs of individual products or orders and to substitute instead pre-determined product unit costs for costing product and inventories. This approach has been found to be the only

---

[1] Specific advantages to be gained are:

    a. Comparisons of actuals with standards, prior to entry in the accounts, are usually limited to details for foremen or executives at the departmental level. Summary cost statements up to and including the profit and loss statement can show comparisons with standards if standards are on the books and variances are collected in appropriate accounts. Thus the use of standards is extended upward to top executives.

    b. The requirement that standard costs be tied in with the book cost controls promotes accuracy and causes both the accounting and operating departments to take them more seriously.

    c. The clerical facilities of the accounting department are utilized to advantage in producing the control reports.

**51**

practical one in some industries where the diversity of products is very great and the individual order of relatively low value. In many other industries this use of predetermined costs is the most economical way to account for manufacturing costs. Savings of clerical expense result primarily from eliminating the need to carry many relatively small variations in actual costs through the work in process, finished goods, and cost of sales accounts. Transfers of production costs from department to department are then made at a standard cost which changes much less frequently than does actual cost. Fluctuations in actual cost need be accounted for only in total. Early cost systems of this type used estimated costs but today standard costs are commonly employed for the purpose.[2] This plan of accounting has the added advantage of bringing the accounting for costs into the concept of managerial control which is based upon the comparison of actual with previously planned results.

Companies which use standard costs in their accounts are not limited to those producing a standardized product for stock. In the field study it was found that of 65 of the 72 companies, 35 stated that they made principally a standardized product for stock, 25 stated that they made principally a product produced to the customer's order or specifications, and five companies stated that their production was about equally divided between stock and special order work.[3]

## Accounting Procedure With Standard Costs

### Extent of Application in Costing

Standard costs may be set and used for all elements of manufacturing cost or they may be applied in accounting for some elements of cost and not for others. Thus of the 68 companies which were interviewed and which use standard costs in bookkeeping, five do not enter standards in the books for some portions of their costs.[4] The remaining 63 companies use standards for all elements of cost and the remainder of the chapter will be limited to a consideration of these companies.

### Costing Finished Goods and Sales

Most companies transfer completed product from work in process to finished goods and cost of sales accounts at standard cost. Hence entries in finished goods and cost of sales accounts are at standard costs. The same method is

---

[2] For a discussion of the difference between estimated and standard costs, see Chapter 1.

[3] Most companies have some work in both the stock and special order categories. Where most work is for stock, there may be production of tools and machines for use in the company's own plant, production of samples and experimental models, or repair and construction jobs. Even though regular production is costed on a standard or actual process basis, a limited amount of job order costing is commonly done for special work.

[4] Of these 5 companies, 2 have only overhead standards on the books although one has complete material and labor standards which are used for control and pricing purposes and the other has material usage standards for cost control. The latter company was in the early stage of developing standard costs at the time of the interview and planned to make more extensive use of standard costs later on. Another company which was also just beginning to use standard costs had no material standards. Material price standards are not used by one company because its product is priced on the basis of material at market price. Still another company has material and labor standards, but uses actual overhead.

usually followed in costing finished parts which are put into stock for subsequent use in manufacturing. Where a single inventory account is in use, the inventory account is credited at standard and cost of sales charged for standard cost of goods sold.

This use of standard costs for costing finished goods and sales has several advantages, namely:

1. The standard cost of products completed and of products sold can be determined immediately without waiting for the actual cost to be calculated. This, in turn, helps to prepare monthly statements in a shorter time than if actual costs were used for the purpose.

2. Where a great many different products are made it may be practically impossible to determine actual costs of each product. By using standard costs, the preparation of profit and loss statements by product lines is facilitated.

3. Some clerical saving may result from keeping finished goods stock records in quantities only. This practice eliminates the necessity for recording actual unit cost of each receipt and issue.

## Costing Work in Process Inventories

Procedures which use standard cost for costing work in process inventories vary widely according to the nature of the industry and the accounting methods of the individual company. Work in process accounts are usually charged with materials at standard price and with labor at the standard rate. Material quantity and labor performance variances are determined at points in the manufacturing process which best facilitate cost control. Entries to remove these variances to variance accounts are based upon summaries of material requisitions, time tickets, scrap reports, inspection reports, etc. Overhead is charged to work in process accounts at the standard rate, based upon the method of applying overhead used by the individual company.[5] Under this plan of applying standard costs the more important variances are transferred to variance accounts before the entry transferring completed goods from work in process to finished goods account is made. Hence the variance which appears when finished goods are cleared from work in process at unit standard cost is usually only a residual of variances not previously separated.

Since the standard cost of a finished product unit is built up by following the sequence of the manufacturing process, it is relatively easy to determine the standard cost of goods at the stage of completion reached at the end of a period. Most of the companies studied take a physical inventory of work in process at

---

[5] In the field study it was found that overhead is usually applied to product on the basis of standard hours or standard dollars. Only a few companies use actual hours or actual dollars for the purpose. Standard hours are preferred to actual hours because the former are not greatly affected by extraneous factors and thus better measure production. As stated by the controller of one company:

"Normal time required to manufacture is the proper medium for assigning overhead. Actual direct labor does not represent normal or actual production time because of different direct labor variances on different product lines. These direct labor variances represent, not productive time, but nonproductive time since they arose from waiting for materials, use of inefficient methods, etc. Little, if any, overhead is applicable to such labor losses and in reality such variances are themselves indirect costs or overhead."

the closing date while others rely upon perpetual inventory records. In the latter case production counts are made at the completion of each manufacturing process and inventory records are kept which show at any time the quantity of work in process and the stage of completion reached.[6] The extent to which each of the above methods is used was not determined in the study.

## Costing Raw Materials Inventories

In the field study it was found that approximately three-fourths of the companies price materials at the standard price when the materials are received. These companies carry their raw materials on the books at standard cost, although in some cases the price variance applicable to unused or unsold material is regarded as an inventory valuation account. Some companies stated that they obtained important savings in clerical expense by eliminating actual prices from stock cards and requisitions. Other companies stated that they found such savings to be insignificant.[7] Pricing material at standard on receipt of the material may have an advantage in that the causes of price variances are more easily determined if recorded at the time they occur.[8] A few companies keep raw material stock records at actual cost because they wish to have actual cost of materials on a detailed basis; other companies obtain approximate actual cost by use of the ratio between actual and standard cost.

## Variance Accounts

When the methods of accounting with standard cost described in the foregoing pages have been applied, the difference between actual costs and standard costs is found in the variance accounts. The number of variance accounts seems to be determined by two considerations:

1. The number and type of variances which are to appear in statements for management use. Most of the control statements are prepared from statistical summaries of original records which underlie the accounts. However, the principal groups of variances commonly appear in the statement of cost of goods manufactured and in the income statement which is prepared for use of internal management.

2. The need for separation of variances to facilitate disposal of the variance balances. Where the different variances are not treated uniformly at the end of the period it may be desirable to have them segregated in the accounts.

---

[6] For an example of this plan, see T. R. Elsman, "Work in Process Inventory Control," N. A. C. A. Bulletin, Sept. 1, 1946, pp. 14-19.

[7] Usually stock ledgers show quantities only, thereby avoiding the necessity for making numerous extensions in terms of dollar cost. However, one company stated that through use of mechanical equipment both quantities and standard cost are recorded on stock cards and by thus eliminating the costing of quantities when a trial balance is taken, clerical expense is no greater than it would be if only quantities were recorded on the stock cards.

[8] Thus a manufacturer of electrical equipment reports that information as to the causes of price variances is useful when variances are written off, when price standards are revised, and when quotations are prepared for customers. When price variances are the result of a general change in commodity prices, revision of the standard prices and perhaps of year-end inventory valuation are usually indicated. When the price variances result from purchase in small quantities or from a higher-priced source in order to obtain immediate delivery, the variances are written off.

Ordinarily the number of variance accounts in the ledger is comparatively limited, for a detailed analysis of variances is not needed for inventory costing purposes.

## Costing of Inventories and Disposal of Variances

In the determination of periodic income, the cost assigned to raw material, goods in process, and finished goods inventories is of prime importance. There exists a divergence of opinion as to whether or not standard costs are proper costs for this purpose. Whether inventories are costed at standard or at approximate actual by companies using standard costs appears to be determined largely by:

1. The type of standards employed.
2. The degree of success which the company has in keeping over-all actual costs in line with standards.

3. The concept held with regard to the kind of cost most suitable for costing inventories.

But whether or not standard costs are used in stating inventories in financial statements, they can be used advantageously to facilitate the determination of inventory amounts. When standard costs are incorporated into the accounts, end-of-period inventories can be stated at standard or converted to actual by the method used in disposing of variances. If the final inventories are to be stated at standard the variances are treated as charges against the current period, while if actual cost is the basis selected the variances are divided between inventories and the cost of goods sold. While methods of making this apportionment differ, the effect is to include with the cost of inventories that portion of the variance which is applicable to the goods in inventory and thereby to arrive at the approximate actual cost of these goods.

In practice a company may treat different types of variances in different ways. Some may be written off in their entirety against the current period while others may be divided between inventories and cost of goods sold.

### Price Standards

Standards employed for material price and labor rates represent three different types of a standard cost. These are:

1. Current standards
2. Normal standards
3. Fixed standards

The effect which the type of standard chosen has on the use of price standards for inventory costing is discussed below.

Since labor rate variances are separated from labor performance variances by only a few of the companies studied, disposal of labor rate variances is discussed with labor performance variances. When labor rate standards are current, the standards are generally kept very close to actual rates paid by revision of the standards when changes in rates are made. Hence labor rate variances are usually relatively unimportant.

## Current Material Price Standards

Current standards are intended to reflect quite closely what the company actually expects to pay for materials.[9] Material price standards of the current type are set either by forecasting what the actual cost is expected to be during the period in which the standard will be in effect or by taking for the standard the actual price prevailing at the date the standard is set. Current material price standards are most commonly reviewed and, if necessary, revised annually although some companies review and change price standards oftener.[10]

## Development of Material Price Variances

The costing of materials in inventories is affected both by the point at which price variances are separated and by the disposal which is subsequently made of the variances. In separating the variances, three methods were found, viz.:[11]

1. Costing materials at standard price on receipt. Companies which follow this method carry all materials in inventory accounts at standard prices. When material price variances are written off currently, as most companies do, the variance is charged against income in the period in which the materials are purchased.

2. Costing materials at standard price when the materials are issued. Under this plan the raw material inventory is carried at actual cost, but work in process and finished goods accounts contain materials at standard price. Price variances are taken into the profit and loss account in the period in which the materials are put into process unless the accumulated variance balance is divided between inventory and cost of goods sold at the end of the period. Companies which use this method wish to separate the material price

---

[9] The field study indicated that most companies use current price standards. Thus in a group of 63 companies having material price standards on the books, the price standards used by 51 companies may be classified as current.

[10] Frequency with which material price standards are reviewed by companies using current price standards is summarized below.

|  | No. of Companies |
|---|---|
| Review standards annually | 33 |
| Review standards semiannually | 2 |
| Review standards quarterly | 3 |
| Review standards monthly | 1 |
| Standards under continuous review and may be changed at any time | 5 |
| Standards reviewed and changed when large variances arise or when it is considered desirable to revise | 6 |
| Standards reviewed for each production order | 1 |
|  | 51 |

[11] The following tabulation shows the frequency with which each of the three methods is used by 51 companies having current material price standards.

|  | No. of Companies |
|---|---|
| Materials costed at standard price on receipt | 36 |
| Materials costed at standard price on issue | 12 |
| Materials costed at standard price on completion of manufacturing process | 3 |
|  | 51 |

variance by product lines and find this aim most readily accomplished by costing material at standard price when the material is put into process.

3. Costing materials at standard price when completed work is transferred to finished goods account. In this case only materials in the finished goods inventory are stated at standard cost on the books, all other materials in inventory being at actual cost. Material price variances are developed in the period in which the goods are completed.

### Disposal of Variances from Current Material Price Standards

When material price standards are, or are intended to be, current standards, three-fourths of the companies interviewed charge off the variances in their entirety in the period in which they are developed while the remaining companies divide material price variances between inventories and cost of sales. In the former case some or all materials in the inventories shown on the balance sheet are at standard price; in the latter case all materials in inventories are costed at approximate actual price.

While the companies which divide price variances have price standards which are intended to be current, a few of them have, during a period of extensive price changes, experienced such large price variances that they considered it necessary to divide the variances between inventories and cost of sales, although they ordinarily treat price variances as period costs. However, most of the companies dividing the variances do so because they prefer actual costs of inventories even though in some cases price standards are revised very frequently and material price variances are negligible in amount. Two of these companies stated that in their cases top management was little interested in standard costs and hence statements prepared for these executives show actual costs and no variances.

### Normal Price Standards

Normal price standards have been described by one writer as:

". . . costing rates which, with historical experience and good judgment as guides, have been predicated on a long-range plan. In this type of costing, the standard rates used for costing labor, material, and overhead are seldom revised. . . . Labor and material standard rates used for costing the labor and material elements of cost are not changed to reflect the inflationary and deflationary effects of prosperity and depression. In other words, the current material specifications and the current labor time standards extended at the normal standard rates are considered to be the normal cost for the labor and material elements of cost." [12]

Actual prices paid at a given time may deviate considerably from the normal standard prices because normal standards are not changed to reflect short period ups and downs in actual prices. However of the eight companies using normal price standards, six had revised their normal material price standards within the year at the time of the field study. These six companies cost inventories of

---

[12] T. R. Elsman, *N. A. C. A. Bulletin,* Dec. 15, 1944, p. 371.

materials at their normal standards and treat price variances as period costs. The remaining two companies having price standards set before 1947 stated that their material price variances were large because their price standards were out of date. For this reason, these variances were being divided between inventories and cost of sales to obtain approximate actual cost of materials in inventories.

### Fixed Price Standards

Fixed price standards are used as an aid in accounting for costs and to measure price trends over a long period. However, when fixed standards are employed, inventories are stated at approximate actual cost rather than at standard cost. Only four of the companies covered in the field study have fixed price standards for material.

Companies which use raw materials fluctuating widely in price sometimes find it advantageous to employ fixed price standards instead of current or normal price standards because it is virtually impossible to keep a current standard up to date or to set a representative normal standard. For example, a manufacturer of storage batteries uses a fixed price standard for lead. Purchases of lead are charged to a materials inventory account at the standard price and price variances are carried to a variance account which is treated as an inventory valuation reserve. Lead used in production is accounted for at standard price in the work in process and finished goods accounts. At the end of each period an adjusting entry is made transferring from the material price variance account to the cost of sales account the amount of the price variance applicable to the quantity of lead in batteries sold during the period.[13] The objective of such an application of fixed standards has been stated as follows by one user of the method.

> "Although price variances are reported currently to management for information and control purposes, the primary use of material price standards is for ease in recording transactions and for valuation of inventories and cost of sales. Moreover, since market prices are available, it is not necessary to use standard material prices in computing costs for selling prices. The material price variance accounts, therefore, are used mainly in computing the amount of variance to be charged monthly against cost of sales . . . and for adjusting standard inventory values to actual on an over-all basis." [14]

The use of a standard price also avoids the necessity for keeping detailed records of prices of material in work in process and finished goods. It thus saves clerical expense and difficulties which arise in accounting for many changes in material prices.

---

[13] See C. E. Carlson, "Standard Costs Under Decentralized Production," *N. A. C. A. Bulletin,* June 1, 1945, pp. 879-886; letter by H. W. Luenstroth in Our Open Forum, *N. A. C. A. Bulletin,* Sept. 15, 1945, pp. 89-90; John F. Mickelson, "Standard Costs Applied to the Manufacture of Silverware," *N. A. C. A. Bulletin,* Dec. 15, 1947, pp. 445-458.

[14] John F. Mickelson, *op. cit.,* p. 450.

Companies employing fixed price standards for one or more major materials commonly use current standards for other materials and for other elements of manufacturing cost. Only two companies were encountered in the field study which use fixed standards for all elements of cost. One of these two companies employs the basic standard cost plan of accounting.[15]

## Material Quantity and Labor Variances

In Chapter 1 it was pointed out that material quantity standards and labor performance standards may represent theoretical ideals, attainable good performance, or an average of unadjusted past performance. Almost all of the companies visited in the course of the field study use attainable good performance standards for material quantity and labor performance. In setting standards for these elements of cost, current control considerations are usually stressed more than the inventory costing questions which are involved. While no specific measure to determine the tightness of standards could be developed in the field study, the general impression gained was that net variance balances are usually relatively small under material quantity standards. On the other hand, net labor variance losses are common and sometimes substantial in amount.

That these standards are generally viewed as satisfactory for costing the material quantity and labor element in inventories can be seen from the following summary of practice derived from the field study. As stated previously, only a few companies separate labor rate variances from labor performance variances and hence the figures below refer to the total labor variance.

| | No. of Companies | |
| | Material quantity variances | Labor variances |
|---|---|---|
| Variances treated as period costs; inventories charged with standard cost only | 47 | 52 |
| Variances divided between inventories and cost of sales; inventories at approximate actual cost | 13 | 11 |
| No standards for this element of cost; actual cost used.. | 3 | 0 |
| Number of companies reporting | 63 | 63 |

Where the variances are divided between inventories and cost of sales, the reason for this practice can usually be ascribed either to the fact that standards deviate substantially from attainable performance [16] or to a managerial preference for actual cost.

---

[15] For a description of this plan, see Eric A. Camman, *Basic Standard Costs,* American Institute Publishing Co., 1932; or *Cost Accountants' Handbook,* Ronald Press Co., 1945, pp. 270-71 and pp. 355-387.

[16] Most of these companies have standards which have not been revised for a number of years. One company is developing a new line of products and has not been able to set what it considers to be satisfactory material quantity standards; hence as a temporary measure it divides the material quantity variances and costs inventories at actual. This company's labor variances are very small and hence it charges off labor variances.

*Overhead Cost Variances*

The standard overhead rate is usually based upon a volume of production which is intended to provide for recovery of overhead costs over a period of years. Used for costing production, it avoids the disturbing effect of fluctuations in production volume which tend to increase unit costs in periods of low activity and to decrease unit costs in periods of high activity. Moreover, since the variable overhead costs are included in the overhead rate at the unit allowance budgeted, incurrence of variable overhead costs in excess of the amount budgeted for the quantity of product made does not increase the cost of goods produced because the excess cost is treated as a variance.

While there are three factors which can cause overhead variances, namely, production volume, production time, and spending, the field study showed that only the total overhead variance is developed on the books. Since none of the companies interviewed make a distinction between the different overhead variances in variance disposal, only the total over- or underabsorbed overhead balance is needed. Analysis of the overhead variance for cost control or other purposes is done off the books.

*Overhead Variance Disposal*

Practice in disposal of overhead variance by the 63 companies covered by the field study is summarized below.

|  | *No. of Companies* |
|---|---|
| Overhead variance treated as period cost.................... | 49 |
| Overhead variance divided between inventory and cost of sales.. | 10 |
| Loss variances treated as period cost, gain variances divided between inventories and cost of sales..................... | 4 |
|  | 63 |

With a few exceptions, companies having overhead standards which are up to date cost inventories at the standard overhead rate and write off variances. Most of these companies review their standard overhead rates once a year or whenever it is considered necessary because of changes in conditions.[17] While overhead

---

[17] Frequency with which standard overhead rates are reviewed was reported as follows:

|  | *No. of Companies* |
|---|---|
| Annually | 43 |
| Semiannually | 3 |
| Quarterly | 3 |
| When considered necessary | 14 |
|  | 63 |

rates are reviewed at fairly short intervals, changes are not always made at each review. The following statement seems to be representative of the point of view held by a majority of the companies interviewed:

"When new burden rates are set they are intended to remain fixed for as long a period as possible, say two to five years. However, changes in production schedules, improvements in manufacturing methods, shifts of production between factories, etc., frequently make it necessary to revise these burden rates more often." [18]

At the time of the field study it was found that all of the 49 companies treating variances as period costs and all but three of the companies using other disposal methods had revised their overhead standards in 1946 or 1947. A number of these companies commented to the effect that in the past the standard overhead rate had been revised only at intervals of several years, but that marked changes in volume and expense factors required revision shortly after the close of the war.

Companies which divide overhead variances between inventory and cost of sales or profit and loss do so because overhead standards are distinctly out of date, because activity substantially above normal has resulted in overabsorption of overhead with the consequence that inventories are stated in excess of actual cost, or because managerial policy in the company calls for actual costs in the financial statements. These companies generally follow the same practice in disposal of direct material and direct labor variances.

### Position of Variances in the Profit and Loss Statement

Writers on standard costs have generally advocated showing variances as adjustments to profit in the profit and loss statements prepared for use of management. Two general patterns can be distinguished in statements which follow this plan. The first, which is used when standard selling prices are used, arranges the items in the statements as follows: [19]

| | |
|---|---|
| Net Sales ............................... | $ xx |
| Budgeted Net Profit .................... | xx |
| Sales Volume Gain or Loss............... | xx |
| Standard Profit on Current Sales.......... | xx |
| Total Variances ........................ | xx |
| Net Profit Before Federal Taxes.......... | xx |

---

[18] John F. Mickelson, "Standard Costs Applied to the Manufacture of Silverware," *N. A. C. A. Bulletin*, Dec. 15, 1947, p. 448.

[19] For illustration of this form of profit and loss statement, see *Cost Accountants' Handbook*, Ronald Press Co., 1945, pp. 62-65.

Analysis of Variances:
> Sales Price Variance ................ xx
> Sales Mixture Variance .............. xx
> Cost Variances (listed in detail)....... xx
>
> Total Variances .................... xx

The second pattern, which does not require standard selling prices, appears in the following form: [20]

> Net Sales (actual) ...................... $ xx
> Standard Cost of Sales—Manufacturing.... xx
>
> Anticipated Gross Profit ................. xx
> Cost of Sales—Commercial ............... xx
>
> Anticipated Operating Profit ............. xx
> Cost Variances (listed in detail)........... xx
>
> Net Profit Before Federal Taxes.......... xx

These forms differ principally in that the first presents an analysis of sales variances in addition to cost variances. In both, emphasis is placed upon the variances and the effect which these variances have had on profits. A statement in this form enables the reader to determine how well costs have been kept in line with standards and when variances have occurred the principal causes for such variances are shown. Such statements may be the best method for bringing to top executives the comparison between standard and actual costs. The methods shown above also seem to follow from the view that manufacturing cost variances are not inventoriable costs.

Another plan of showing variances in the profit and loss statement incorporates them with the sales and cost of sales sections of the statement. This method of presentation follows the usual practice of charging manufacturing cost variances to cost of goods sold.[21] That the method of pricing followed may also be a consideration in determining the presentation of variances can be seen in the following comment received from one accountant interviewed in the field study:

> "If it is customary to take actual cost into consideration when the selling prices are quoted it would appear to me more logical to adjust the cost from standard to actual before comparing it with the selling prices. If, on the other hand, selling prices are based entirely on standard cost, it may be logical to apply the variance as an adjustment of gross profit."

The separate presentation of variances is of value principally to management and normally they are not shown separately from other costs in statements pre-

---

20 See Clinton W. Bennett, "A Case Study of Small Business Controls," *N. A. C. A. Bulletin,* April 15, 1948, p. 1013.

21 The field study showed that in all but four cases variances are charged to cost of sales at the end of the year by companies costing inventories at standard cost.

pared for stockholders, creditors, and others not engaged in active management of the company.

When inventories are stated at actual cost, variances are viewed as part of the costs of manufacturing. Hence the portion of the variances which is related to goods which have been sold is logically added to standard cost of sales and the remainder is added to standard cost of inventories.

## ADJUSTMENT OF INVENTORIES COSTED AT STANDARD COST

### Revision of Costing Standards

When the accounting plan uses standard costs for costing inventories and sales, it is desirable to review the standard costs periodically and to make changes in the costing standards when it is found that the standard costs in use are no longer proper ones for the purpose. The field study indicated that most companies review their standard costs annually, usually during the latter part of the fiscal year. Necessary changes in the standards which will be used for costing production during the coming period are made at this time.

This procedure may be contrasted with the need for more or less continuous revision of standards used for cost control. For the purpose of cost control, changes in product specifications or manufacturing methods which result in changes in operation time standards, material usage standards, or overhead budgets are commonly made during the year in order that these standards may serve as guides in day-by-day operation of the plant. However, for reasons of clerical economy, these interim changes are usually made only in the detailed operation standards and are not carried all the way through to the standard cost of the finished product until the end of the year when a complete revision of standard costs is made. When changes are made in some component details of the product cost standards without changing the latter standards, a variance will arise from the difference in charging goods into work in process at one standard cost and taking them out of work in process at another standard cost. These variances can be written off during the interim periods until a revised finished product cost standard is established.[22]

---

[22] Practice in treatment of these variances from interim changes in standards differs according to the size and importance of the variances. One company which finds its variances from this cause to be small states that "We do not attempt to determine the variance, but simply allow the overages and shortages to accumulate in the inventory account, and adjustment is made at the end of the year at the same time that the books are adjusted to the physical inventory." Another company separates the amount of its labor variance due to changes in standards, describing its procedure as follows:

"In order to determine the amount of the variance, the productive labor tickets are sorted to part number and operation number, and compared with the cost books. Differences are summarized departmentally in hours. Extension of these hours by the departmental standard labor rates determines the amount of labor variance from standard. In addition, these hours are used to adjust the time allowed hours at actual in order to convert them to standard for burden absorption purposes."

Another company prepares a complete monthly analysis of variances in which the amount of variance due to changes in control budgets is determined.

Changes in price and labor rates are sometimes handled by use of an inventory valuation account. The objective here is to bring the cost of the closing inventory into line with current conditions without adjusting the detailed underlying records.[23] However, the field study indicated that most companies make a complete revision of standard costs once a year. In the process, variances which resulted from changes in control standards without corresponding changes in costing standards are wiped out and standards used for the two purposes are brought into agreement.

### Adjustment of Inventory to New Standard Costs

Changes in the standard costs raise the question of whether or not to adjust the closing inventory to reflect the changes that have been made in the standard costs. The answer to this question seems to depend upon the nature of the change that has been made in the standard costs.

1. If the new standard costs reflect conditions which affected the actual cost of the goods in the closing inventory, most companies adjust the inventory to the new standard cost and carry the contra side of the adjusting entry to cost of sales by way of the variance accounts. In effect, this procedure assumes that the standard costs used to cost goods in the inventory have been incorrect and that restatement of inventory cost is needed to bring inventories to a correct figure on the books. Since the use of incorrect standards has affected the variance accounts as well as the inventory, the adjustment is carried to the variance accounts.

2. If the standard costs represent conditions which are expected to prevail in the coming period but which have not affected costs in the past period, closing inventories are costed at the old standards. It appears to be common practice to adjust the detailed inventory records to new standard costs before the end of the year just passed. In order to maintain the control relationship which the inventory accounts have over subsidiary records, the same adjustment is entered in the inventory control accounts and the contra entry is carried to an inventory valuation account. Thus the net effect is to state the inventory in the closing balance sheet at old standard costs. In the next period the inventory valuation account is closed to cost of sales when the goods to which the reserve relates move out of inventories. By use of this technique, the detailed records can be adjusted to new standards before the beginning of the year while at the same time the net charge to cost of sales in the new period is for old standard cost since the latter cost was correct at the time the goods were acquired.

### Other Inventory Adjustments

Inventories which have been costed at standard cost are subject to the usual adjustments for obsolescence, physical condition, and realizable value. Most of the companies interviewed follow a policy of stating inventories at the lower of cost or market. In many cases any reduction of book costs to a lower market

---

[23] This method may be explained more specifically by assuming that a general increase in labor rates has taken place during the year. If standard costs have not been revised, the labor variance account will reflect this increase in wages paid. If desired, the amount of this variance applicable to inventory can be transferred to an inventory valuation account and the reminder of the variance charged to cost of sales since it is the amount of the increased labor cost applicable to goods which have been sold. On the books the inventory valuation account is used in order not to destroy the control relationship between inventory accounts and subsidiary records, but in preparing the balance sheet the valuation account is consolidated with the inventory.

figure is accomplished in the process of adjusting inventories to revised standard costs. Thus a decrease in material price is reflected in the new standard cost at which the closing inventory is stated. However, if standard costs used in costing the closing inventory do not meet the requirements of lower of cost or market, an adjustment to reduce standard cost to market value can be made. In general, the use of standard costs for costing inventories would seem to offer no new problem in this respect, for the test of a comparison with market prices can be applied to standard costs as readily as it can be applied to actual costs.

### Disclosure of Standard Costs as a Basis for Inventory Costing

When published financial statements disclose the fact that standard costs are used for costing inventories, the information is ordinarily given in connection with an explanation of the basis used for valuation of the inventories appearing in the balance sheet. Thus one company has appended to its balance sheet the following footnote:

> "Raw materials and supplies were priced at the lower of actual cost or replacement market of specific items (on a first-in, first-out basis); in process at standard costs (approximate actual); finished goods at the lower of standard cost or replacement market."

In another case the balance sheet contains the following:

> "Inventories priced at standard costs..................... $xxx."

In the same report the auditor's certificate states that:

> "Such quantities were priced, in accordance with the policy consistently followed by the company, at standard costs, which exclude certain overhead costs."

### CONCLUSION

This chapter shows that standard costs are useful in accounting for production costs because they facilitate reduction of clerical expense by eliminating the need for carrying the many variations in actual costs through the inventory accounts. When standard costs are used in accounting, these fluctuations in cost are diverted to variance accounts, accumulated there, and disposed of in total.

With the above plan of accounting, production is costed at standard cost. A majority of the companies interviewed state their inventories at standard cost and charge the variances against income of the period in which the variances arise. They justify this practice on the grounds that variances represent inefficiency, avoidable waste not recoverable in selling price, and random fluctuations in actual cost. As such, these variances should be treated as period costs rather than as costs of goods in inventories. This reasoning seems to require standards which are current and attainable. Changes in external factors such as prices or changes in methods and performance efficiency which are made or accepted by management require revision of standards used in costing.

Standards which are not current still have value in reducing the clerical expense of bookkeeping for costs. However, in this case the general practice is to divide the variances between inventories and cost of goods sold or profit and loss thereby converting both inventories and cost of sales to approximate actual costs. In making this adjustment consideration is given to under- or overabsorption of overhead.

# Chapter 4

## STANDARD MANUFACTURING COSTS FOR PRICING AND BUDGETING

**P**REVIOUS chapters have dealt with standard costs for cost control and for costing inventories. There remains to be considered the use of standard costs in pricing and budgeting. Costs for these purposes must be predetermined costs since decisions in the fields of pricing and budgetary planning are made before the costs under consideration are incurred. They also need to be flexible enough to meet new conditions that arise and reliable enough to serve as dependable guides to management. Standard costs are especially valuable for these purposes to the extent that they are predetermined costs based upon a careful study of what can be accomplished with the production facilities available. Such standards are also readily adjusted to reflect anticipated changes in prices of material and labor, production methods, or volume.

### Standard Manufacturing Costs for Pricing

Pricing is essentially a management problem rather than an accounting problem. In order to set selling prices, executives who make pricing decisions need information about the relevant factors, one of which is costs to make the goods to be sold. Furnishing these costs is regarded as an important function of the accounting department in most of the companies whose practices were used as the basis for this study of standard costs. This chapter is concerned with the kinds of costs which are furnished to management for price making purposes. It will not consider the question of how selling prices are actually set.

Replies as to the kind of costs supplied for pricing were received from 67 of the 72 companies. Of these, 62 companies make use of standard costs in pricing.[1] A number of companies commented to the effect that the use of standard costs saves clerical work in preparing cost information for pricing purposes and makes costs available to pricing executives more quickly than would be possible if standard costs were not available. As stated by one writer:

"Since standard costs represent the cost that should be attained in a well-

---

[1] The remaining 5 companies make no use of standard costs in connection with pricing. At the time the field survey was made, one of these companies had standard costs which had not been revised since before the war and use of standard costs had been largely discontinued until such time as they could be brought up to date. The other four companies stated that cost is not a consideration in pricing their products. However, one of these companies does use its standard costs to estimate gross profit by product lines as a check upon its pricing.

organized plant operated at normal capacity, they are ideally suited for furnishing information as to costs of manufacture which will enable the sales department to properly price its products to the trade.

"The use of standards eliminates the necessity for innumerable factory tests, which are otherwise required to provide the basic data for the building of cost estimates for the sales department. Cost estimates based upon factory tests or past averages are bound to vary more or less and may in no instance represent the cost that should be attained under normal operating conditions." [2]

## Responsibility for Pricing

Costs are supplied to the department or persons responsible for pricing decisions. Location of this price-making authority varies according to the organization plan of the individual company. However, the sales department or some executive in the sales department was mentioned by most companies as receiving the cost information prepared for pricing purposes. Hence it appears that in most of the companies the sales department is in possession of information concerning the standard costs of manufacturing the goods sold. In a number of these companies costs prepared for pricing purposes are also supplied to various top executives not concerned exclusively with sales. Thus the president, vice presidents, treasurer, and controller were frequently mentioned.

Some companies reported that pricing was done outside the sales department and that the price data is supplied to the persons who determine prices. Thus two companies have a "price making" department, one company has a pricing committee, and in several other companies various executives set the prices.

## Nature of Product and Method of Selling

The preparation of costs for pricing is influenced by the nature of the product sold and the methods of selling it. Companies selling standard products manufactured for stock usually publish their prices and therefore need costs for pricing only when new catalogs or discount schedules are being prepared.[3] Since catalog prices usually remain unchanged for a period and repeated sales are made at the same price, costs used in setting catalog prices must be representative of what the company can do on a continuing basis during the life of the price schedule. On the other hand, companies which sell special products manufactured to the customer's specifications need an estimate of cost each time they prepare a quotation. In this case every order raises a pricing problem and the cost department will be continually engaged in estimating costs for pricing purposes. Owing to these differences in the problems, the following discussion will be broken

[2] E. A. Green, "Practical Standards—Their Development and Use," *N. A. C. A. Bulletin,* Feb. 1, 1935, p. 652.

[3] However, in several cases comments were received to the effect that current variances are watched as an indication of possible need for price revisions. This applies particularly to raw material prices and to labor rates.

down into two sections covering, respectively, the use of standard costs for setting catalog prices and the use of standard costs for bid prices on individual orders.

In the group of 62 companies using standard costs in pricing, 51 have catalog prices and 41 have bid prices on special orders. Both catalog prices and bid prices were reported by 30 companies and hence these companies are represented in both categories. On the other hand, 21 companies have only catalog prices and 11 companies have only bid prices.

## Standard Costs for Catalog Prices

Companies which have catalog prices can be divided into four groups in respect to the type of cost figures which they supply to pricing executives. These groups are composed of:

1. Companies which supply pricing executives with standard costs without application of any adjustments to the standards.
2. Companies in which costs supplied to the pricing executives are standard costs adjusted by the ratio of actual cost to standard cost as shown by the variance accounts.
3. Companies which use current market prices for materials, and in a few cases for labor, together with standard costs for other elements of product cost when preparing pricing costs.
4. Companies which adjust their standard costs to reflect actual costs which are anticipated during the period for which the prices are to be in effect.

It will be seen in the discussion below that these different procedures are often merely different ways of arriving at approximately the same concept of cost for pricing purposes.

## Unadjusted Standard Costs for Pricing

Out of 51 companies which have catalog prices for some or all products, 13 stated that the standard costs which they supply for pricing are the same standard costs used for cost control and inventory costing purposes. No adjustments to cost standards used for pricing are made for variance account balances or for current market prices. However, the standard costs used by these companies are current in every case, the standards being reviewed and, if necessary, revised once a year or even oftener.[4] Thus the practice of these companies appears to be to bring the standard costs up to date each time new catalog prices are prepared.

## Standard Costs Adjusted for Variances

It was found that 21 of the 51 companies having catalog prices adjust their standard costs by the ratio of actual cost to standard cost in preparing costs for

---

[4] It may be interesting to note that one company in this group has two sets of standard costs, one of which is used for the purposes of pricing and cost control and the other used for inventory costing. The material and labor standards used for cost control and pricing are kept continuously up to date by making changes at any time necessary. Standard costs of material and labor used for inventory costing are revised only once a year. The standard overhead rates which are used both for pricing and inventory costing purposes were set 12 years ago and have not been changed since.

pricing purposes. This point of view has been expressed in the accounting manual of one company as follows:

> "It is necessary, in order to operate at a profit, to establish our sales prices sufficiently high to cover those variances which we are unable to eliminate."

With a few exceptions, these companies have material price and labor rate standards which are not revised frequently enough to be close to current actual costs. A majority of the companies in this group revise their standard costs annually, but some revise irregularly. Thus several companies were found to be using standard costs set from 3 to 10 years ago, and these standard costs deviated very substantially from actual costs at the time the field study was made. Material usage and labor performance standards are, in some cases, kept tight relative to actual performance and hence these companies find that sizeable net debit balances are likely to appear in the variance accounts.

Companies adjusting standard costs for variances often have standard costs which are developed primarily for inventory costing purposes. In order to avoid the clerical expense entailed by frequent changes, the standard costs are revised only once a year. Changes in costs which take place during the year show up on the books as variances and through adjustment of costing standards by the variance ratio, approximate current costs are obtained for pricing purposes. When costs for pricing purposes are prepared by this method it may be necessary to develop variances by products or types of products since an over-all variance ratio may not be appropriate for different products.

### Standard Material Costs Adjusted to Current Market Prices

Five out of the 51 companies having catalog prices adjust material price standards to current market prices when using costs for pricing purposes. All of these companies produce products in which such raw materials as cotton, copper, or steel make up a large portion of the total cost. In these industries selling prices tend to follow raw material prices quite closely. Hence costs used for pricing are composed of current market price of the raw material plus standard labor and overhead needed to convert the raw material into a finished product.

### Standard Costs Adjusted for Anticipated Changes

In the group of 51 companies having catalog prices, 12 companies adjust standard costs to reflect anticipated changes in costs. Here the aim is to price on the basis of future costs rather than upon past or present costs. As expressed by a writer on the subject:

> "The catalog on which the sales department is working is the new season's catalog—not the old one. The price-fixing authority wants to know what products *will* cost not what they *did* cost. . . .
>
> "Now let us see how standard costs meet this problem. Let us assume that our standard costs were set nine or ten months before and in the interim there

have been changes in raw material prices and labor rates. Obviously these standard costs cannot be used for future price fixing. But observe that in order to figure these standard costs we had to make certain preparations. We had to determine the exact specifications of each product and compute the normal requirements of each constituent material, on the basis of normal yields, or wastage, and we had to establish normal time allowances for each operation. All of these were set down on a standard cost card or sheet. These quantity figures were extended at the normal prices or cost rates prevailing at the time the new year's standard costs were established. They are *now* available for pricing at *today's* prices and rates, or at the forecast normal prices and rates for *any* projected future period.

"... Even though a change in normal production level may be forecast, the fixed and variable parts of the costs have been identified so that new normal rates may be computed without additional research." [5]

The standard costs used by these 12 companies vary from standards which are virtually current actual costs to standards which were obviously not current at the time of the interview. Adjustment of standard costs to reflect expected material prices and labor rates is made by all 12 companies. A few of these companies also make adjustments for efficiency expected and in some cases forecasted actual overhead is used in costs prepared for pricing.

### Standard Costs for Bid Prices on Individual Orders

Products priced on a bid basis may be standard items, but perhaps more often they differ in some respects from products made before. In some instances they are entirely new. However, there are usually parts, materials, or operations which are the same as those used in products previously made. The existing standards are thus usually applicable in estimating costs of special or new products, although there may be a greater margin of error in such estimates than there is in cost estimates for products concerning which more experience is available.

When preparing bid prices, it might be expected that pricing executives would need more detailed information about the components of cost and how these components vary than when setting catalog prices on standard articles. This expectation is borne out by the results of the field study which indicate that most of the 41 companies pricing on a bid basis build up cost on each order or request for price from the detailed standards.[6]

---

[5] George D. McCaffrey, "The Swing to Standard Costs," *The Arthur Andersen Chronicle*, July 1947, pp. 164-65.

[6] The extent to which standards are so used by these 41 companies is tabulated below:

|  | No. of Companies |
|---|---|
| Use quantity standards to estimate material and labor requirements of order | 39 |
| Use material price and labor rate standards to estimate cost of material and labor of order | 36 |
| Use standard overhead rate to estimate overhead cost of order | 37 |

In each case, the remaining companies out of the 41 reporting do not use standards for these purposes.

Standard costs are usually used without adjustment when standards are current and variances are small in comparison with the margin of gross profit. However, about half of these 41 companies adjust the cost developed from the detailed standards to approximate actual in the process of compiling costs for bidding. Whether or not this adjustment is made seems to be determined partly by the type of standard cost in use and partly by the policy followed with respect to the kind of costs wanted for price making purposes.

Companies using standards which are infrequently revised adjust standard costs to approximate current actual levels for pricing purposes. This is usually done by applying the appropriate current variance ratio to the standard cost of the product, although material price standards are adjusted to current market levels by several companies. While definite information was not obtained, it appears likely that companies which maintain quite tight standards for purposes of cost control also adjust these costs by throwing back some or all variances when preparing cost estimates for pricing.

Companies which adjust standard costs to approximate actual costs for pricing purposes sometimes make an exception for the overhead element. In these cases the standard overhead rate is used without adjustment while variance ratios are applied to material and labor standards. Only 7 companies stated that they make any separation between fixed and variable portions of the costs used for pricing purposes. It thus appears that the marginal income approach to pricing is little used by the companies interviewed, for the separation of fixed and variable costs needed for this type of cost analysis is provided by only a few companies.

### Effect of Order Size

An additional adjustment to standard costs used as a basis for special order price quotations is made to incorporate in pricing costs any effects which the size of the order is expected to have on manufacturing costs of the order. Such an adjustment is made by approximately two thirds of the companies reporting pricing on a bid basis.[7]

This adjustment is usually determined by the specific circumstances that cause costs to vary with order size. For example, where machine setup, tooling, or engineering costs differ from the allowances made for these items in the standard costs, the standard costs are adjusted to reflect the expected actual cost of the order.[8]

---

[7] Several companies which report no adjustment to standard costs for order size adjust the markup percentage instead of the standard cost.

[8] A manufacturer of sheet metal stampings separates its overhead costs into two groups and has two overhead rates. One of these, used to apply general plant overhead, is used without adjustment in preparing costs for pricing. The other rate is used to apply overhead which is special to the product on order and covers amortization of product development costs, setup costs, costs of special tools and dies, and other costs associated directly with specific orders. These latter expenses are applied at a rate based upon either the estimated quantity of a product to be sold or upon the number of units ordered by a customer.

### Comparison of Actual and Estimated Costs

Approximately two thirds of the reporting companies make comparisons between estimated costs used for pricing and actual costs of manufacturing goods for special orders. In some cases these comparisons are made only occasionally or on large orders. Apparently most of these companies rely upon their manufacturing cost variance reports for control of costs and compare costs estimated for pricing with actual costs principally to check upon the accuracy of their estimating procedure. Other companies compare estimates with actual costs on every order. In some instances the estimate of cost prepared for pricing becomes the control standard for the order and variances are developed on a job order basis.

### Conclusion—Standard Costs for Pricing

This study shows that when standard manufacturing costs are available, these standard costs are generally utilized for pricing purposes. Where standards represent performance which the company expects to attain and prices which it expects to pay for material, labor, and services, standard costs are used for pricing without adjustment. On the other hand, where anticipated changes in costs are not already incorporated in the standard costs or where standards do not cover all the costs which the company expects to have to incur to produce the goods, standards are adjusted accordingly. While variances are separated from standard costs for cost control purposes and, by many companies, excluded from inventories in accounting, an average provision for unavoidable variances is commonly included in costs used for pricing purposes.

### STANDARD MANUFACTURING COSTS FOR BUDGETING

Budgets are used for planning and coordinating future activities and for controlling current activities. The present study considers budgets developed primarily for the first of these purposes. Moreover, the study is limited to the way in which standards are used in preparing manufacturing cost budgets.

While this standard cost study as a whole has been based upon practice of 72 companies only 39 of these companies have budgets for planning and coordinating their activities in which use is made of standard costs. Hence the following conclusions are based upon practice of these 39 companies.

### Preparation of the Budget

Preparation of the budget begins with a forecast of sales. Using this forecast of sales together with the inventory desired, production requirements for the coming period are set up. Once the quantity of goods to be produced has been ascertained, the next step is to determine the cost to manufacture these goods. Such a calculation of manufacturing costs is needed to provide the cost of sales and inventory figures in the budgeted statements. Since budgets are based upon estimates, past experience, or upon standards, the accuracy of the resulting budget will obviously be influenced by the reliability of the data which is used in establishing the budget in the first place. Where standards are available they provide a ready means for translating the budgeted production figures into manufacturing costs.[9] The results are also likely to be more reliable than when standard costs are not available. As stated in Chapter 1 with respect to the use of standard costs in preparation of a budget:

"The reliability of standard costs stems from the fact that they have been based upon careful studies of material usage requirements, operation methods and times, variability of cost with volume, and the best arrangement of equipment. Furthermore, the standards have been tested and performance under them has been recorded so there is a good basis for predicting what performance can be expected in the future.

### *Forecasting Variances from Standard Costs*

Standards used to control operating performance are often tighter than expected actual performance so that a net debit variance usually is anticipated. Variances from standard or normal volume and perhaps variances from standard cost prices which will be in effect during the coming budget period may also be anticipated. In order that budgets may reflect expected actual results, a majority of the companies interviewed forecast variances from standard costs when preparing their budgets. In the group of 39 companies, 28 companies forecast variances while 11 companies do not do so. As stated by one company:

"The standards set for standard costs are not always attained, due either to failure to procure the normal volume or mixture of sales, or the failure to conduct our activities on a basis that resulted in the attainment of standard allowed performance. The final financial budget will therefore include an estimated amount indicating these anticipated variances."

These forecasted variances are, to some extent, an indication that standards for control are kept tighter than estimates used for planning. They also represent allowances for standards which have not been revised to give effect to expected actual conditions. This is often true of overhead volume standards and to a lesser extent of other standards.

The companies which do not forecast variances follow either of two procedures which give results which are essentially the same. In the first case, a forecast of purchase prices and volume is made for purposes of the budget. New standard costs are then set on the basis of the forecast. On the other hand, some companies first revise their standard costs and then use the revised standards to prepare the budget. With both methods standard costs and budgets represent what the company expects to accomplish and no variances are planned.

---

9 Several of the companies interviewed which prepare a budget but do not use standard costs for this purpose budget cost of sales as a percentage of sales. In these cases no detailed breakdown of manufacturing costs is made for purposes of the budget.

## Budgeting Material Requirements

The budget for direct material requirements is built up from the material quantity standards and the forecasted production of each product. On this basis a purchasing schedule is prepared in order to have needed material available at the proper time. These purchases enter into the cash budget. Total cost of material to be used, regardless of whether it is to come from present inventory or future purchases, becomes an element of cost of goods to be manufactured.

A majority of the companies reported use of their material quantity standards for this purpose without modification or adjustment. However, in a few cases where standards are not current or variances have been large some allowance is added to or subtracted from the standard in budgeting material requirements.

Quantities of material required must be priced in order to obtain the aggregate material cost for the budget. Where material cost price standards have been recently revised and represent current or forecasted prices, the price standards are commonly used for the purpose. However, a number of companies use current market prices for material or adjust price standards before using them in budgeting material cost. In the latter cases price standards usually do not reflect price changes which are anticipated in the coming budget period.

## Budgeting Labor Requirements

Labor requirements are usually budgeted in terms of the number of manhours and type of labor force that will be needed. These figures are obtained in most cases by using labor standards to calculate the time required to produce the goods called for by the production schedule. One writer has described the procedure of his company as follows:

"Another very important estimate which is directly related to the production budget is the forecast of labor requirements. The chief purposes of a labor budget are:

1. To enable the personnel department to provide workers when and where they are needed.

2. To minimize labor turnover and the losses it causes in time, money, and efficiency.

3. To facilitate the estimating of cash requirements for payrolls.

"For many years we have maintained statistical data showing the standard direct labor hours required in each production, inspection, and assembly department to manufacture every model in the various lines. The sources of this information are the make-up records of each model and the operational cost cards. With such information it is possible, within a few hours' time, to determine the number of direct labor hours needed in each department to produce the entire production schedule for the budget period. By adjusting these figures to account for operators' efficiency, absenteeism, scrap, etc., we can make an estimate of the number of hours required in each department to produce the schedule.[10]

---

[10] Robert Walker, "Synchronized Budgeting in the Business Machine Industry." *N.A.C.A. Bulletin,* August 1, 1947, pp. 1457-58.

In a number of cases adjustment of standards by the current labor performance variance ratio was reported. Since debit labor variances seem to be quite common, it might be expected that such an adjustment would be considered desirable, for the planning budget stresses expected accomplishment.

In determining the cost of budgeted labor time, companies which revise labor rate standards concurrently with the preparation of the budget use their rate standards, but most companies use current or anticipated labor rates in place of standard rates.

### Budgeting Overhead

In preparing the master budget most of the companies interviewed use their standard overhead rates for determining the cost of goods to be produced in the budget period. However, if budgeted volume differs from the volume used in setting the standard overhead rate, some under- or overabsorbed overhead must be allowed for in the budget.

A majority of the companies interviewed break down manufacturing expense into fixed and variable categories in order to aid them in planning allowable manufacturing expenses for the budgeted volume of production. This breakdown is to be found in the flexible budget standards which have been established to control manufacturing expenses. The amount of variable expense is generally taken from the flexible budget, although adjustment for changes in prices and wage rates may be made if these factors are not reflected in the standards. On the other hand, if volume of production called for by the budget is less than that used in developing the overhead standards, fixed expenses are often reviewed, since an indicated volume variance loss can sometimes be reduced by managerial decisions with respect to size of the organization to be maintained and other expenses which are fixed principally by managerial policy.

### Relationship Between Planning and Control Budgets

The planning budget sets the goal for the coming budget period. In order that the manufacturing costs may be kept within bounds anticipated by the budget plan, it is necessary that continuous control be exercised over costs during the budget period. The standard costs (including the flexible overhead budgets) serve this function when the standards which were used in construction of the budget are subsequently used for current control.

While actual costs seldom can be kept exactly in line with either standards or budget, it is possible to collect and analyze the variances in order to show what caused these variances. In this process two comparisons are made, viz., (1) actual cost with standard cost, and (2) actual cost with budgeted cost. The first comparison serves as a measure of current success in control of manufacturing costs while the second shows how successful management has been in operating in accord with the plan set up by the budget. Variances from control standards must, of course, be kept within limits set by any forecasted variances if the budget is to be met.

Reports showing actual costs in comparison with budgeted costs provide management with data which aid in determining when action should be taken to bring performance into line with the budget or to modify the budget. A record of experience expressed in variances from the budgets of previous periods is also helpful in improving the accuracy of future budgets.

### Conclusion—Standard Costs for Budgeting

In the field study it was found that most of the companies which use budgets for planning and coordinating activities employ their standard costs to aid in estimating the costs of manufacturing the goods called for by the budget plan. Standard costs are especially useful for this purpose because they are predetermined product costs ascertained by careful study of cost performance. However, standard costs are commonly based upon normal volume and efficient use of production facilities while budgets reflect expected actual performance under the conditions anticipated. Hence it is usually necessary to include a forecast of variances from standard costs in the budget. By making such a forecast of variances the standard costs can be utilized in building up the cost figures called for by the budget and then adjusted in total by the amount of the variances forecast. In those cases where no forecast of variances is made, the standard costs are revised to incorporate in them the conditions which would otherwise produce variances.

# Chapter 5

## A STANDARD COST CASE STUDY

PREVIOUS chapters have stressed the various uses of standard costs and have shown how standards serve each purpose. They have described the prevailing practice in the use of standard costs by the 72 companies which were interviewed in the field study. The manner in which the various uses of standard costs are coordinated and the desired information for each purpose is obtained from a single set of standards and cost records remains to be shown.

Identical procedures for this purpose are not applicable in all businesses and the approach to a coordinated use of standards must be made through methods which are adapted to the circumstances of the individual company. It seems that this aspect of the study of standard costs can be best presented in the form of a case study which shows how one company has accomplished such objectives. The methods of the company chosen for this case study are not necessarily the best possible, but they do provide an example of an operating system in which standard costs are used for all of the purposes of cost control, costing production, pricing, and budgeting. Furthermore, in this company management is provided with cost information which it finds highly valuable in directing activities of the business and this information is obtained at what it considers to be a reasonable expense for record keeping.

### The Company and Its Product

This report presents the standard cost system of The Drybak Corporation, a company which manufactures a variety of trousers, coats, and vests for hunting, work, and other uses. Products manufactured by the company are approximately equally divided between those for stock and those made to order of the customer. They usually comprise from 200 to 250 separate articles at a given time. An important characteristic of the business is the continuously changing design of a diversified line of products. Individual production orders are comparatively small and many different orders are in process at a given time. For this reason the company uses a job lot plan of manufacturing. The company has one plant and normally operates with a force of 350 employees.

### Uses of Standards

The company makes initial use of its standards for preparing price quotations. Subsequently, the same standards are employed for planning production in the factory, for controlling costs of manufacturing to facilitate accounting for costs, and in preparation of the annual budget. Cost of goods in inventory is stated at standard manufacturing cost.

The present costing plan using standard costs has been developed gradually over a period of 14 years. It replaced a previous system under which historical costs were accumulated by job orders. According to estimates of the company's treasurer, accounting expenses under the standard cost plan are substantially lower than they would be under the older plan. In addition, standard costs provide a wealth of information which management can use in operating the business. Much of this information would not be available at all without standard costs.

### Setting Standard Costs

Requests for quotations and orders from customers specify the garment desired, its design and material, and the quantity of each size. If the item has not been manufactured before, a standard cost is set as a basis for a price quotation. These standard costs are developed from a careful analysis of the material required, labor operations to be performed, and the overhead applicable. While the garment desired usually differs in some respects from any made previously, operating characteristics of the equipment used are known. Likewise the combination and sequence of manufacturing operations required differ according to the specifications of the product, but these processes are widely used in many types of garment making. Consequently records of past experience and time study standards for the operations to be performed enable the company to set a reliable standard cost to use in pricing.

The cost changes for each change in garment size but the selling price is the same so the standard cost is based on an average size. Thus, coats ranging in size from 37 to 49 have a standard cost set on the average size which might be size 43. Variations in costs may occur on individual orders because of a heavier demand for larger or smaller sizes, but in the long run these variations even out.

When an order is received, the manufacturing data sheet (Exhibit 1) based on a dozen garments is made up. The description and the material quantity standards are shown on the front of the sheet, and on the back are listed the operations to be performed and the standard allowed hours required. The information on this sheet is then carried over to the standard cost record sheet (Exhibit 2) on which the standard cost is developed by costing the materials and labor at standard rates.

When the garment desired by the customer has been manufactured previously a standard cost is already available since the standard cost record sheet described above will have been prepared at some earlier date. Complete files of these standard cost records are maintained for this purpose. Procedures followed in setting

**COATS**
**MANUFACTURING DATA SHEET**

LOT NO.

COAT DESCRIPTION Hunting
Regular corduroy

4 Buttons - setting on face

Plain shoulders

Hinge adjustable - W/B and B Hole

2 Stitch down muff pockets

BARTACKS

| | DATE | | PCS. | PATTERN NO. |
|---|---|---|---|---|
| COLLAR | | | | 4501 |
| UNDER COLLAR | | | | |
| FRONT | | | | 5016 |
| FRONT FACING | | | | |
| BACK' | | | | 6091 |
| SLEEVE | | | | 7350 |
| POCKET | | | | 8540 |
| POCKET | | | | |
| POCKET | | | | |
| POCKET | | | | |
| FLAPS | | | | |
| FLAPS | | | | |
| FLAPS | | | | |
| FLAP LINING | | | | |
| FLAP LINING | | | | |
| FLAP LINING | | | | |
| CUFFS | | | | |
| CUFF LINING | | | | |
| SLEEVE LINING | | | | |
| BODY LINING | | | | |
| SHO. PADS | | | | |
| SHELL LOOPS | | | | |
| GAME PKT. | | | | |
| ENT. FLAPS | | | | |
| ENT. LININGS | | | | |

| CODE NO. | MATERIALS | WIDTH | QUANTITY | CODE NO. | MATERIALS | UNIT | QUAN. |
|---|---|---|---|---|---|---|---|
| 23 | 11 oz. Army Duck | 40" | 40 | 610 | Size ticket | M | 12 |
| | | | | | 36/E Br. buttons | G | 108 |

| OUR NO. | CUSTOMER | LOT NO. | LABELS | PACKAGING | P. R. CHANGES |
|---|---|---|---|---|---|
| | | | | | |

EXHIBIT 1

**STANDARD COST RECORD**

| DESCRIPTION | | | | | DATE | | CUSTOMER | | STYLE NO | |
|---|---|---|---|---|---|---|---|---|---|---|
| Hunting Coat | | | | | SIZE SCALE 37–49 | | SIMILAR TO | | CODE NO. | |
| DIRECT MATERIALS | | | | | STANDARD COST PER DOZ. | | ESTIMATED | | ESTIMATED | |

| CODE | DESCRIPTION | WIDTH | QUANTITY | PRICE | EXTENSION | PRICE | EXTENSION | PRICE | EXTENSION |
|---|---|---|---|---|---|---|---|---|---|
| | BODY MATERIALS | | | $ | $ | $ | $ | $ | $ |
| 23 | 11 oz. Army Duck | 40" | 40 | .65 | 26.00 | | | | |
| | TOTAL | | | | 26.00 | | | | |
| | TRIM | UNIT | | | | | | | |
| 610 | Thread | | | | .93 | | | | |
| 420 | Size Ticket | M | 12 | .80 | .01 | | | | |
| | 36/E Br. Buttons | G | 108 | .60 | .45 | | | | |
| | TOTAL | | | | 4.00 | | | | |
| | TOTAL MATERIALS | | | | 30.00 | | | | |
| | TRANSPORTATION IN | | | % | | % | | % | |

| LABOR & EXPENSE | COST CENTER | RATE | SAH | EXTENSION | SAH | EXTENSION | SAH | EXTENSION |
|---|---|---|---|---|---|---|---|---|
| CUTTING | .58 | 2.00 | 1.00 | 2.00 | | $ | | $ |
| SEWING | 51 | 1.50 | 12.00 | 18.00 | | | | |
| INSPECTION | .80 | 1.50 | .50 | .75 | | | | |
| TOTAL LABOR & EXPENSE | | | | 20.75 | | | | |
| STANDARD MANUFACTURING COST | | | | 50.75 | | | | |
| ADMINISTRATION | | | | | | | | |
| SELLING—CHAIN—JOBBER—RETAIL | | | | | | | | |
| PROFIT & LOSS | | | | 9.00 | | | | |
| TOTAL STANDARD COST | | | | 59.75 | | | | |
| COMMISSION % | | | | | | | | |
| DISCOUNT % | | | | | | | | |
| MARK-UP % | | | | 5.30 | | | | |
| STANDARD SELLING PRICE | | | | 65.05 | | | | |

EXHIBIT 2

standard costs for products made for stock and for products made to special order of the customer are identical.

Orders received are broken down to economic lot sizes to be processed in the factory. Since many different orders are always in process at the same time, careful planning and scheduling of production is necessary. Operation time standards are essential for this purpose.

### Material and Labor Cost Standards

The material quantity standards for the major materials of the garment are determined by the use of templets or patterns designed for the average size chosen. These templets are arranged to give the best usage of the material, and the standard yardage is determined from these areas plus an allowance for end pieces and lappings. This standard is shown on the lower left-hand side of the manufacturing data sheet (Exhibit 1). Standard quantities for the miscellaneous items of material such as buttons, zippers, tags, purchased pockets, etc. are obtained by inspection of the garment and are listed on the lower right-hand side of the data sheet. The standard material quantities are transferred from the manufacturing data sheet to the standard cost sheet (Exhibit 2), where they are multiplied by standard prices. Standard material prices are determined by annual forecast of the cost of material to be purchased, tempered by the inventory on hand at the time the forecast is made.

The labor operations to be performed on the garment are found by careful analysis of the laying out of templets, the material cutting and trimming, the sewing, pressing, inspecting, etc. By studying these operations in the light of recorded motion and time study data, standard times can be determined and entered on the standard cost record sheet. Standards set by this method for pricing purposes are temporary but are used until additional orders are received. Then they are revised by study of actual time on the previous order. The final labor time standards are also used as the basis for an incentive wage payment plan.

Operation time standards are summarized in standard hours for each of three departments, viz., cutting, sewing, and inspection. The time to process a dozen garments of the specified design in each department is entered on the standard cost record and extended by the standard hourly rate for labor and overhead expense combined. The standard labor rate is the average rate being paid at the time the standards are set.

### Overhead Cost Standards

Standard hourly overhead rates for each cost center or department are determined by dividing the standard allowed hours at the practical production capacity of the department into the budgeted expense for the department. The budgeted expenses are taken from the flexible budget for each department and to these are added the prorated general overhead expenses budgeted. Some of the rates for the stitching centers have been found to be so nearly alike that they have been averaged, and only three rates are used. The selling, administrative, and all other expenses are applied to the job using a standard rate times the manufacturing cost. The standard cost sheet is completed by adding the mark-up to the cost to determine the selling price. Flexibility in pricing to meet competition can be obtained by varying the mark-up figure.

### Cost Control—Material Costs

Standard costs for pricing would be of little value unless the actual costs were kept within the standard costs. When prices have been based upon the expectation that the goods can be made for the standard cost, any unfavorable variance results in a decreased profit. Hence the company takes the same standards developed for pricing and applies them for the control of costs during the process of manufacture. Control of costs has been maintained within about one per cent, above or below standard. This would seem to represent both good standards and successful control.

The factory is made cost conscious by keeping the standards before the shop personnel and by promptly following up off-standard performance. For example, in the cutting department, if the marker finds that he is going to exceed the standard yardage of cloth allowed, he checks with his supervisor to determine whether it is best to go ahead or to try to rearrange the templets to meet the standard. Quantity variances in use of body material for garments occur mainly in the arrangement of templets for sizes other than the average size upon which the standard cost is set. Since it is possible to bring such variances to the attention of the proper authority before the material is cut, a decision can be made as to whether to use additional labor in rearranging the templets or to use more than the standard quantity of cloth. Markers are highly skilled and carry a relatively high hourly rate whereas some materials are expensive and others are cheap. A control plan which thus enables the decision to be made before the variance occurs can often avoid substantial overruns in the cost of an order.

The cost of materials is controlled through the standards appearing on the standard cost sheet (Exhibit 2). Control methods have been adapted to the different types of materials. Thus for the body material, a card for the shop job is issued to the cutting department showing the article, style number, order number, kind of material, and the standard quantity needed. When the job is to be laid out and cut, the card is the basis for the issue of material. An excess length of cloth of the correct width is issued to the cutting department. The material is lapped for the required layers and length as determined from the standard layout for the required sizes, marked from the templets and cut. The extra lengths are then returned to the stockroom with a statement of the remaining yardage in the roll. The card issued to the cutting department is marked with the material issued, the amount returned, and the difference or net yardage actually used. Any errors in the yardage of the material returned will be picked up when the material is reissued on another job. These shop cards are not convenient for filing and analysis purposes since they are often received in poor condition and a great number are required for some jobs. Hence the quantity and cost of body material used are summarized on the card shown in Exhibit 3.

This card is made out for each shop order and is identified through the information at the left end and by the method of punching. The actual material usage is obtained from the shop card, while the standard is obtained from the standard cost sheet. The actual yardage is extended at the standard price and compared with the standard cost, the difference being recorded in the upper right-hand corner. These cards can be thumbed through each day to pick out large variances, or the variances can be tabulated.

The other materials, with the exception of thread, are issued in standard quantities determined by the standard cost record sheet. From the latter a bill of materials is prepared and issued to the storeroom where a clerk measures and assembles the items in a box which goes along with the body material. The standards allow for losses of about one per cent on certain items and hence favorable usage variances can be obtained. If, due to loss or breakage, the standard quantity is not enough to complete the order, a requisition for additional materials must be made out by the department supervisor. This requisition calls the supervisor's attention to the variance. The requisitions are collected by departments and charged to material usage variance accounts at the end of the month. No attempt is made to charge these variances against specific job orders since they are so small as to be negligible.

Thread is a comparatively small item of cost and is controlled by monthly comparison of the actual cost of the quantity issued for all orders with the corresponding standard cost. It can thus be seen that control of the major items in material cost is by individual shop order while the other items are controlled by periodic comparison of actual cost with standard cost.

### Cost Control—Direct Labor

Control procedures for direct labor costs, like control procedures for material costs, are adapted to the operations performed in each department. Large labor variances are expected in the cutting department and, for this reason, the actual time consumed in marking, laying, and other operations in this department are recorded by jobs. This is done by entering the hours used on the back of the material shop card and then summarizing the data on the card shown in Exhibit 3. Actual hours, standard hours, and the variance in hours are shown in the column headed "cutting time." A space at the right-hand side of the card has been provided for the dollar amount of the variance, but this information is not filled in because it has not been found useful. Control is applied by use of the variance in hours rather than in standard dollars. This control is exerted on the day that a shop order is completed in the department, a matter of approximately a day after the job is started by the cutting department.

| CUTTING TIME | | |
|---|---|---|
| MARK | 4 | 0 |
| LAY | 15 | 2 |
| CUT | 12 | 2 |
| TRIM | 15 | 1 |
| SHADE MARK | | |
| TOTAL | 46 | 5 |
| STANDARD | 52 | 0 |
| VARIANCE | 5 | 5 |

DATE CUT 2/18/48
CUT NO.
TRIM NO.
OUR STYLE NO.
CUST. STYLE NO.
QUANTITY 52

**MATERIAL VARIANCE**

| CODE | WIDTH | STD. YDS. | ACT. YDS. | PRICE | EXTENSION |
|---|---|---|---|---|---|
| 23 | 40" | 2080 | 2100 | .65 | $1365 00 |

924.58 — MAT'L $13 00

925.58 — LABOR $

ACC'T $

ACC'T $

TOTAL ACTUAL MATERIAL $1365 00

TOTAL STANDARD MATERIAL 1352 00

TEST G/L
TRIM NUMBER TENS UNITS
STYLE NUMBER THOUSANDS HUNDREDS TENS UNITS
CUT NUMBER THOUSANDS HUNDREDS TENS UNITS

DATE CUT YEAR 48 47 46 45 MONTH 7 4 2 1

FORM C.

EXHIBIT 3

Employees in the sewing and inspection centers are paid largely by piece rate and time tickets show only the standard time. Variances arise when actual daily time is greater than allowed time for the production attained, due to slow work, lost time on repairs, etc. Since variances on these operations are relatively small, the actual labor cost is compared with the corresponding standard cost on a weekly basis instead of on a shop order basis.

### Cost Control—Overhead

Overhead costs are controlled through the use of flexible budgets. The budget for each department contains only those expenses which are controllable by the executive in charge of the department. These expenses are composed principally of labor, machine parts, and materials which are accounted for as indirect charges to product, but which are directly chargeable to the specific department. No pro-rated expenses are included in the budgets, but general plant overhead, which includes such items as power, light, office expense, vacation pay, depreciation, etc., is budgeted separately and is controlled on an over-all basis.

The flexible budget for each department is set up by accounts and is classified into fixed, variable, and semivariable components. By thus separating the fixed

## THE DRYBAK CORPORATION
## COST AND VARIANCE STATEMENT
### FACTORY

Center Name _____ No. ____

| Account | Extra Budget Allow. | Current Allow. | Actual | Var. | Year to Date | |
|---|---|---|---|---|---|---|
| | | | | | Actual | Variance |
| Direct Labor | | | | | | |
| Other Labor | | | | | | |
| Total Direct Labor | | | | | | |
| | | | | | | |
| | | | | | | |
| Total Indirect Labo | | | | | | |
| Machine Parts | | | | | | |
| Shop Indirect Materials | | | | | | |
| | | | | | | |
| Department Total | | | | | | |

Keyman

| Activity (Volume) | Production | Standard | Effy. Ratio | T.C. Ratio |
|---|---|---|---|---|
| Current | | | | |
| Year to Date | | | | |

| Recovery | Month | Year to Date |
|---|---|---|
| Standard Budgeted Recovery | | |
| Recovery at Indicated Activity | | |

EXHIBIT 4

portion from the variable portion, the total allowable amount for each item can be determined for any level of activity by adding to the fixed amount the rate per hour for variable expense times the standard hours. Weekly comparisons between budgeted and actual indirect labor and monthly comparisons for other budgeted expenses are made. A report (Exhibit 4) is prepared listing variances.

Due to the presence of fixed costs, the amount of overhead charged to production agrees with the amount budgeted only when the plant operates at practical capacity. Differences between the budgeted overhead and the absorbed overhead arise when actual volume differs from practical capacity and these differences are volume variances. The volume variances are reported by departments and for the factory as a whole in a variance summary for top management (Exhibit 5). The recovery of fixed expenses is reported to each department for information only, since top management is considered responsible for volume variances.

Extra budgetary allowances are made to cover expenses of a major nature which were not foreseen at the time the department budget was set up and over which the supervisor responsible under the budget has no control. For example, the company used the wage rates then in force when the budget for 1948 was prepared. Subsequently wage rates were increased. The supervisor was then given credit for the increase in his labor costs by entering the amount in the column marked "extra budgetary allowance" on the form shown in Exhibit 4. The total allowance thus is determined by adding this extra allowance to the usual allowance based on the budget. The net difference between actual expenses and the total allowance constitutes the variance for which the supervisor is responsible. Extra allowances are also shown on the variance summary statement (Exhibit 5) since they constitute deviations from the budget which have been approved by management.

### Cost Control—Selling, Administrative, and Other Expenses

To control selling, administrative, and other expenses a flexible budget similar to the manufacturing overhead budget is used. Sales dollars instead of standard allowed hours are used to measure activity. In the same way, the actual expense and current budgeted allowance are compared by items for control of cost performance, and the budget and charge to profit and loss are compared for the variance due to volume of sales. Variances are summarized and shown on the variance summary.

### Reporting Cost Information to Management

One of the most important features of any cost control plan is the reporting of information about costs and variances to the persons responsible for the costs. Since top management of this company is so close to detail operations, formal reports are kept to a minimum. Thus the cutting department cards shown in Exhibit 3 are used for current control purposes by sorting out those cards show-

| | | | THE DRYBAK CORPORATION | | | |
|---|---|---|---|---|---|---|
| | | | VARIANCE SUMMARY | | | |
| Cost Center | Direct Labor | Other Control | Extra Budget. Allow. | Volume | Total | Total Year to Date |
| 51 Breech | 173 | 85 | | -64 | 194 | |
| 52 Wool Coat | -72 | -104 | | -215 | -391 | |
| 53 Duck Coat | 90 | 37 | | 126 | 253 | |
| 54 Hats & Caps | 36 | 73 | | 89 | 198 | |
| 56 Training | -48 | -37 | | -49 | -134 | |
| 57 Woodfield | 141 | 90 | | 212 | 443 | |
| 58 Cutting | 65 | 40 | | 35 | 140 | |
| 59 Inspection | 23 | 35 | | 24 | 82 | |
| 61 Factory-General | | -247 | | 316 | 69 | |
| | | | | | | |
| Total | 408 | -28 | | 474 | 854 | |
| | | | | | | |
| 01 Admin. | | 327 | | 154 | 481 | |
| 02 Compt. | | 115 | | 96 | 211 | |
| 03 Samples | | -236 | | 32 | -204 | |
| 10 Procurement | | 78 | | 63 | 141 | |
| 62 Rent | | 145 | | 175 | 320 | |
| Total | | 429 | | 520 | 949 | |
| | | | | | | |
| 11 Sales | | -297 | | 216 | -81 | |
| 12 Shipping | | 140 | | 185 | 325 | |
| Total | | -157 | | 401 | 244 | |
| Grand Total | 408 | 244 | | 1395 | 2047 | |

| RATIOS | Month | | | Year to Date | | |
|---|---|---|---|---|---|---|
| | Volume | Efficience | Total Cost | Volume | Efficience | Total Cost |
| Manufacturing | | | | | | |
| Administrative | | | | | | |
| Sales | | | | | | |
| Total | | | | | | |

| RECOVERY | | | | | |
|---|---|---|---|---|---|
| By Inventory | | | Non-Inventory | | |
| Cost Cent. | Month | Year to Date | Cost Cent. | Month | Year to Date |
| 51 | 12,320 | | 01 | | |
| 52 | 7,655 | | 02 | | |
| 53 | 11,912 | | 03 | | |
| 54 | 1,836 | | 10 | | |
| 56 | 825 | | 11 | | |
| 57 | 6,419 | | 12 | | |
| 58 | 5,565 | | | | |
| 59 | 2,872 | | | | |
| 61 | 6,940 | | Total | | |
| 62 | 3,790 | | | | |
| | | | P & L | | |
| Total | 60,134 | | Total | | |

EXHIBIT 5

ing variances. These cards also form a valuable record of cost experience which is much used in preparing standard costs for new orders.

A weekly departmental payroll summary (Exhibit 6) is sent to supervisors. Departmental, general factory, selling, administrative, and other expenses are reported monthly to the executives responsible for control of these expenses on the form shown in Exhibit 5. Using the principle of exceptions, the monthly profit and loss statement (Exhibit 7) shows only the variances and their effect on profit rather than the details of actual costs. The budgeted net profit is the profit determined at the beginning of the year. By adjusting this profit for the volume gain or loss due to change in sales income plus the change in overhead absorption, the standard profit for the actual sales is determined. The actual net profit is computed by adjusting the standard profit by the total of the other variances. An analysis of variances is shown in a section of the statement which follows the net profit before federal taxes.

### Use of Standards in Accounting for Costs

To simplify the accounting procedure, one inventory account is used for raw materials, work in process, and finished goods. This eliminates the need for any transfer entries while goods are on hand. All charges to the inventory account for materials, labor, and overhead are at standard cost. Thus incoming material is debited to inventory at standard price and any purchase price variance entered in a price variance account. Material usage variances are removed from the inventory account to variance accounts, the entry being based upon a summary of the records on which variances are reported.[1] Labor and overhead costs are debited to inventory at standard rates for standard hours produced, with the difference between these debits and credits to payroll and expense accounts being carried to variance accounts.

Perpetual stock records for all raw materials are maintained in terms of quantities only. Stock cards showing quantities of finished goods on hand are also kept. By pricing quantities at standard manufacturing cost, the company's inventory can be determined in a comparatively short time.

When finished goods are shipped to customers, a transfer from inventory to cost of sales is made, using the standard manufacturing cost of the articles sold. The product costs used for this purpose are obtained in the process of setting standard costs for pricing. While the more important differences between standard and actual costs on each order are recorded on product cost cards shown in Exhibit 3, these differences are charged in total to variance accounts and it is not necessary to carry numerous variations in actual cost through the inventory account and its subsidiary records. Control over costs is exercised at the source and in this process comparisons between actual results and standards are made by inspecting or by summarizing subsidiary records. Hence the collection of both

---

[1] These records are the material usage data on Exhibit 3 and the requisitions for material in excess of standard quantity.

## PAYROLL SUMMARY

| VARIANCE | | ACCOUNT | EX. B. ALLOW | | CUR ALLOW | | ACTUAL | |
|---|---|---|---|---|---|---|---|---|
| | | MEASURED DIR. LAB. | | | | | | |
| | | EXCESS ALLOW CONTROL | | | | | | |
| | | | | | | | | |
| | | MAKE UP | | | | | | |
| | | REPAIR & SHOP LOSSES | | | | | | |
| | | | | | | | | |
| | | EXECUTIVE | | | | | | |
| | | SUPERVISION | | | | | | |
| | | FLOOR HELP | | | | | | |
| | | CLERICAL | | | | | | |
| | | SUPPLIES CLERK | | | | | | |
| | | | | | | | | |
| | | JANITORS & WATCHMEN | | | | | | |
| | | TRAINING PROGRAM | | | | | | |
| | | PATTERN | | | | | | |
| | | EXPERIMEN. & SAMPLES | | | | | | |
| | | INSTRUCTION | | | | | | |
| | | SHIPPING LAB. | | | | | | |
| | | TRUCK DRIVER | | | | | | |
| | | STOCK EXPENSE | | | | | | |
| | | OTHER LABOR | | | | | | |
| | | MACHINE MAINT. LAB. | | | | | | |
| | | OVERTIME | | | | | | |
| | | VACATION PAY | | | | | | |
| | | HOLIDAY PAY | | | | | | |
| | | | | | | | | |
| | | | | | | | | |
| | | TOTAL PAYROLL | | | | | | |
| | | | | | | | | |

| % ACT. | UNIT | PRODUCED | BUDGETED | % ACT. | |
|---|---|---|---|---|---|
| COST CTR. | ACT. HRS. | | COST CTR. | | |
| WEEK ENDED (OR MONTH OF) | | | | | |

### COMMENTS

EXHIBIT 6

| Month | THE DRYBAK CORPORATION<br>PROFIT & LOSS STATEMENT | Year to Date |
|---|---|---|
| 235,610 | Net Sales | |
| 20,500 | Budgeted Net Profit | |
| 2,358 | Volume Gain or Loss | |
| 22,858 | Standard Profit on Current Sales | |
| 773 | Total Variances | |
| 23,631 | Net Profit before Federal Taxes | |
| | ANALYSIS OF VARIANCES | |
| -570 | Mark Up (or Down) | |
| 230 | Variety Made & Sold | |
| -340 | Total Mark Up & Variety | |
| 408 | Direct Labor | |
| -28 | Factory Expense | |
| -157 | Selling Expense | |
| 429 | Administrative Expense | |
| 652 | Total Controllable | |
| 390 | Purchase Price | |
| 136 | Material Usage | |
| - | Extra Budgetary Allowance | |
| -65 | Profit & Loss Net Variances | |
| 461 | Total Uncontrollable | |
| 773 | Total Variances | |
| | PROFIT & LOSS INCOME & CHARGES | |
| | Discount Earned | |
| | Anticipation Earned | |
| | Profit on Sale of Assets | |
| | Discount Allowed | |
| | Anticipation Allowed | |
| | Interest Paid | |
| | Social Security Taxes | |
| | Reserve for Bad Debts | |
| | Budgeted Income & Charges | |
| | Profit & Loss Net Variances | |
| | RATIOS | |
| 9.1 | Profit to Sales – Standard | |
| 10.0 | Profit to Sales – Actual | |
| 104.7 | Sales Activity | |
| 101.6 | Manufacturing Activity | |

EXHIBIT 7

actual and standard costs in the accounts can be limited to the data necessary for preparation of financial statements. The company thereby avoids much book-keeping work which would otherwise be required for entering unit costs in per-petual inventory records, distribution of labor costs to orders, and routine pro-ration of overhead to departments and to job orders.

The company reviews all standard costs annually preceding the annual closing which is made on November 30. Revisions in standard costs are put into effect with the beginning of the new fiscal year on December 1. Any adjustment of inventory cost occasioned by changes in standard costs is made through use of an inventory valuation reserve which is subsequently closed to cost of goods sold. Since subsidiary stock records are kept in quantities only, little clerical work is required in adjusting inventory records to reflect changes in standard costs.

A policy of valuing inventories at the lower of standard cost or market is followed by the company. Variances from standard costs are charged to cost of sales monthly, and inventory in monthly statements is at standard cost.

### Relationship Between Budget and Standards

At the end of each year a budgeted profit and loss statement for the coming year is prepared. The anticipated sales income based upon market conditions and tempered by plant capacity is determined by top management. The large amount of special order work together with the changing design of products makes it impossible break down the budgeted sales into quantities of specific products. Hence the production budget is built in terms of standard hours.

The flexible budgets in use are reviewed and revised to incorporate anticipated changes in prices and operating methods. Using the forecasted standard hours of activity and the standard rate per hour for labor and overhead, the expected amount of these elements of manufacturing cost can be inserted into the budget. Material costs cannot be built up from product cost standards because it is not possible to predict what specific articles will be manufactured. Hence the over-all cost of material for the purpose of the budget is determined by subtracting the net profit plus labor and overhead from the forecasted sales income.

No variances are forecast in the budget, for it is expected that the standards will be met by actual operations.

### Conclusion

This case study illustrates an application of standard costs which has success-fully met management's needs in a company characterized by special order pro-duction and many changes in product design. The plan of cost record keeping is also simple and economical.

This company's needs for costs begin with preparation of price quotations. Using established labor time and overhead cost standards together with material requirements of the garment in question, a predetermined cost is obtained for pricing purposes. Since this cost figure is built up by costing individual manufacturing operations which are used in making the goods called for by the order, these detailed costs are used as standards with which to control manufacturing costs. Control over all major items of cost is exercised at the source by providing factory personnel with the standard for each operation to be performed and with prompt reports on actual performance relative to the standards. These reports are simple and, in most cases, informal. Financial reports stressing the effect of variances on anticipated profits keep top executives informed as to the effectiveness with which cost control is being maintained. These reports stress the causes of deviations from the budget rather than actual amounts spent for various purposes.

Use of the standard costs for costing production and inventories avoids the necessity for carrying numerous variations in actual costs through the cost records, a practice which requires substantially less expense for bookkeeping than would be needed if actual costs were accumulated by job orders. Closing inventories are costed at standard, although these standard costs are subject to adjustment to the extent that such costs are not recoverable in future sales.

Standard costs are kept current by annual revision. In connection with the preparation of the budget for the coming year, standard costs are reviewed in order that they may serve as controls over performance in carrying out the operating plan contained in the budget.

## List of Companies Participating in Study of Standard Costs

The following companies were among those participating in this N. A. C. A. research study by contributing information regarding their use of standard costs. The remaining companies preferred that their names not be listed.

American Asphalt Roof Corp.
American Hard Rubber Co.
American Smelting & Refining Co.
Animal Trap Company of America
Armstrong Cork Co.
Arms Textile Manufacturing Co.
A. Schrader's Son
Atlas Powder Co.
Avon Sole Co.
Bridgeport Fabrics, Inc.
Bridgeport Thermostat Div.
    Robertshaw-Fulton Controls Co.
Bryant Electric Co.
Carrier Corp.
Cambridge Paper Box Co.
Chase Brass & Copper Co.
Columbia Mills, Inc.
Commonwealth Shoe & Leather Co.
DeLaval Separator Co.
Dennison Manufacturing Co.
Drybak Corp.
Eagle Pencil Company, Inc.
Eastman Kodak Co.
E. W. Carpenter Manufacturing Co.
Fasco Industries, Inc.
Federal Bearings Co., Inc.
Forbes Lithograph Manufacturing Co.
General Electric Co.
Gilbert & Barker Manufacturing Co.
Goodall Rubber Co.
Hamilton Watch Co.

Henry G. Thompson & Son Co.
Hyde Manufacturing Co.
International Silver Co.
Intertype Corp.
Keystone Watch Case Div.,
    The Riverside Metal Co.
Lehn & Fink, Inc.
Monroe Calculating Machine Co.
Neptune Meter Co.
Permatex Company, Inc.
Pitney-Bowes, Inc.
Reed-Prentice Corp.
Ritter Company, Inc.
Rockbestos Products Corp.
Sargent & Co.
Scovill Manufacturing Co.
Scranton Lace Co.
Sidney Blumenthal & Co., Inc.
Strathmore Paper Co.
S. Stroock & Co., Inc.
Textron, Inc.
Trumbull Electric Manufacturing Co.
United-Carr Fastener Corp.
Veeder-Root, Inc.
Western Electric Co.
White & Wyckoff Manufacturing Co.
Whitin Machine Works
Wickwire Spencer Steel Div.,
    Colorado Fuel & Iron Corp.
York Corp.

# Part II

# VARIANCE ANALYSIS

Published originally as NAA Research Report 22
*The Analysis of Manufacturing Cost Variances*

# CONTENTS

# INTRODUCTION

*Standard costs tell what costs should be and actual costs tell what costs have been. Variances constitute a connecting link between standard costs and actual costs. Since management's goal is operation of the factory at standard cost, significant deviations from standard cost signal the need for managerial attention to conditions which are the source of variances. As a basis for deciding what action should be taken, management should know who in the organization carries responsibility for the variances, what has caused them to arise, and perhaps what effect they have had on product costs. This report presents the results of a study designed to show what the accountant can do in providing management with information which will aid in appraising the significance of manufacturing cost variances.*

The literature of standard costs has emphasized methods for establishing standards and techniques for coordinating standard costs with actual costs through variances. Methods for analyzing variances and the purposes served by such analysis have not been described with equal thoroughness. This report dealing with the analysis of manufacturing cost variances therefore supplements the Association's earlier series of research reports devoted to standard costs. Since the earlier study covered the nature of and uses for standard costs, this subject is not discussed here. The reader is referred to the report presenting results from the prior study for a treatment of these topics.[1]

In this study, twenty-seven companies employing standard costs were interviewed to determine how variances from standard costs are analyzed and what benefits are realized from such analyses. In addition, records of field interviews carried out during several other N.A.A. research studies were drawn upon for material not previously published. The emphasis of this study has been placed upon methods employed by those companies which were judged to be making most effective use of standard costs. For this reason, the report stresses practices and viewpoints of a comparatively small group of the companies interviewed. This approach has been selected because it seems likely that members of the Association will find the most advanced practices to be more useful than those practices which are most commonly found.

---

[1] N.A.A. Research Report entitled "How Standard Costs Are Being Used Currently."

# THE ROLE OF VARIANCES
# IN COST CONTROL

Control over current costs must obviously be exercised before the fact rather than after the fact. Preventive cost control depends upon actions taken at the point where losses and waste can occur, or where savings can be made. This type of control uses basic operating standards expressed in terms of material specifications, operation methods and times, preferred equipment and facilities. Such standards need to be current at all times—i.e., they must represent the methods which should be followed when the work is done. Among the companies which were judged to be making effective application of standard costs for cost control, comments were often made to the effect that such standards "are under continuous review and are changed whenever necessary." In the words of a member of the Committee on Research:

> "Standard costs serve no purpose unless the accountant is able to sell management on the merit of an installation sufficient in scope whereby manpower is provided to review and change standards whenever necessary."

Since variance are measures of performance under standards, the standards must first be good in order to yield reliable measures of performance.

While the primary aim of management should be to obtain compliance with standards, perfection cannot be obtained in either standards or practice and some variances will always arise. Past losses from failure to meet standards cannot be retrieved, but the study of variance is an important step toward improving performance in the future.

However, before management can take effective action to realize the opportunities for improving control over costs, it needs to know not only the amount of variance, but also where the variances originated, who is responsible for them, and what caused them to arise. In other words, analysis is necessary to bring out the significance of the variances in terms of sources, responsibility, and causes. When such analyses are combined with an appropriate plan of reporting, management can rely upon the principle of exceptions to disclose problems calling for attention without laborious study of many detailed facts and figures.

2

# ANALYSIS OF VARIANCES
# BY RESPONSIBILITIES

Control over cost must be applied at the place and time where the cost originates. For this reason, a basic fundamental in the design of a cost system is that each cost be charged initially to the responsibility within which the decision to incur the cost is made. The same cost may subsequently be allocated to other cost centers in determining product costs, but for purposes of cost control the individual who has authority to incur a cost should be held responsible for that cost. In commenting on this, one member of the Committee on Research stated:

> "To me, this is by far the most important result to be obtained from modern standard cost systems. Under responsibility accounting, the responsible operator is actually given a piece of the business to run as though it were his own. How he performs, determines what results he will obtain."

## Definition of a Responsibility

As defined by one company, ". . . a responsibility is an organizational unit engaged in the performance of a single function (or a group of closely related functions) having a single head accountable for activities of the unit." In this company a responsibility is established wherever the amount of cost involved or the type of operation performed makes control economically desirable and where analyses of costs as compared with standards are frequently required. A responsibility set up for cost control purposes may coincide with a cost center established to collect costs for assignment to products or it may include several such cost centers. Functional cost groups which serve solely as cost collecting centers do not constitute responsibilities.

## Accounting for Costs by Responsibilities

An organization in which there is clearly defined authority and corresponding placement of responsibility is a prerequisite to effective control over costs. Delegation of authority and placement of responsibility—in other words, the development of an organization—is a management function. On the other hand, measuring the costs incurred and reporting variances from standards assigned to each responsibility is a cost accounting function.

3

The first step toward accounting for costs and variances by responsibilities is to prepare a cost classification in which area of responsibility established by the company's organization plan constitute the primary basis for classifying both standard and actual costs. As described by a writer on the topic:

"Each department, as a responsibility unit, is charged with all costs over which it has control. (For the purpose of product costing, costs over which the organizational unit has no control are also allocated to it.) As represented in its controllable costs, each department thus has its own accounts. Within the department these accounts are further classified according to function. The number of such departmental accounts depends on the nature of the expense and the extent to which the expense can be classified and controlled."[2]

Inasmuch as the matching of standard and actual costs takes place as the costs are accumulated by responsibilities, the analysis of variances by responsibilities is a "built in" feature of the cost system. Reports showing standard costs, actual costs, and variances for each responsibility are ordinarily produced as part of the clerical routine of accounting for costs.

When introducing standard costs, it is necessary to make sure that the classification of accounts permits accumulation of cost by responsibilities. Where standard costs have not been in use, it is usually found that the accounting system has been designed primarily for determining product costs and that costs controllable by two or more supervisors are merged in a single account. Under these circumstances, revisions in classification and coding must be made.

*Placing Responsibility for Variances*

Some factors affecting manufacturing costs can be quite readily standardized and controlled through the use of standards. Usage of direct materials, direct labor, and certain variable overhead items usually fall in this category. The usage of these cost factors is generally controllable by management at the plant operations level. Responsibility for costs arising directly in productive departments is then clearly assignable to supervisors of the respective departments.

However, the field study showed that management often finds it difficult to define responsibility for costs which originate in service departments and which are subsequently allocated to productive departments. Among the companies interviewed, those which seem to be most successful in establishing responsibility for service department costs utilize plans which differ somewhat according to the nature of the service and the conditions under which it is rendered. The differences can be outlined as follows:

---

[2] A. J. Penz, "Standard Costs in a Small Steel Company," *N.A.A. Bulletin*, July 1951, pp. 1348-9.

1.  When the volume of service to be provided is fixed by decision of executive management rather than by supervisors in charge of centers in which the cost is absorbed, no responsibility for control is attached to allocated charges. For example, productive department foremen are not responsible for costs allocated to their departments for such services as cost accounting, production control, personnel, engineering, air conditioning, and other similar functional services. Here responsibility for the amount of service provided rests with executive management, for it has authority to determine how extensively such functions are to be developed. Expenditures made for such services are, on the other hand, a responsibility of the heads in charge of the respective service departments. Expenditures to be made by each of these departments are budgeted and the department head is held responsible for operating within his budget. Most costs in such budgets are considered fixed, with the amount allowed being proposed by department heads and approved by top management as proper to provide the kind and amount of services desired. However, variable components are present in some instances—e.g., clerical costs in one company's production control department.

2.  The costs of continuously available services such as power, steam, compressed air, and similar items whose consumption fluctuates with daily activity in the factory are usually charged to the consuming department at a standard unit rate when methods for measuring services consumed by individual departments are available. Responsibility for the quantity consumed, but not for the unit cost of the service, is then placed with the supervisor in charge of the consuming department. Where the consumption of such services by individual departments is not measured, supervisors of the latter departments are usually not held responsible for costs of the services used. On the other hand, the unit cost of such service is a responsibility of the service department head. Since there is usually a substantial fixed component in costs of rendering the service, a flexible budget is used and responsibility for control stresses costs variable with output of service. Measures of performance are sometimes expressed in phyical units, as for example, in a power plant where energy produced per pound of coal is employed.

3.  Services rendered on demand (e.g. services of millwrights, mechanics, electricians, etc.) are charged to consuming departments at a standard hourly rate. Budgets of consuming departments ordinarily contain an allowance for such services and the department head is responsible for variances from this allowance. The costs of rendering such services are covered by departmental budgets similar to those employed for other departments. However, expenses in these budgets

tend to be rough estimates because it is seldom practical to set standards for the type of operations performed. Most companies admitted that clear-cut placement of responsibility for maintenance and repair costs had not been achieved, but that methods described above had demonstrated considerable value. As an illustration, one company stated that foremen had become conscious of service costs and had tended to avoid unnecessary calls for such service since the practice of charging for such services was instituted. Other examples were also provided by companies interviewed to indicate that savings can be obtained by attempting to place responsibility for costs. In one of these examples, a general tightening of control over maintenance employees' time followed complaints by foremen even though such complaints were sometimes without foundation.

The field study seems to indicate that assignment of responsibility for control of service costs is often distinguished from allocation of these costs for costing products. In general, accounting allocations are unsatisfactory for fixing responsibility for costs. As stated by the representative of one company in describing his company's experience, the practice "results in a chronic argument about fairness of the charges." The reason is that bases of allocation which are "equitable" for cost finding purposes are often not directly related to short period fluctuations in controllable costs.

Notwithstanding the fact that there are inherent difficulties in setting standards for some manufacturing activities and that any plan for cost control has practical limits, experience of a few companies shows that judicious attempts to place responsibility for both direct and indirect costs have yielded savings.

*Separation of Operating and Non-Operating Variances*

In order that variances assigned to supervisors in charge of departmental operations may be limited to variances from costs controllable by these supervisors, additional variances are needed to screen out the effect of cost changes for which management at this supervisory level is not responsible. For example, price and volume variances are needed because management responsible for the quantities of materials and services consumed in manufacturing is not also responsible for variances due to changes in market prices and for the volume of orders received by the factory. Another example is furnished by the practice of setting up special variances to segregate the effect which shortages of materials and the necessity for using substitutes have had on costs in some of the companies interviewed.

These variances usually reflect outside influences impinging on the company's operations and the company must adapt itself to existing conditions since it cannot control the causes of the variances. Authority to deal with such problems rests with top management and is exercised by initiating

6

changes in products, methods of manufacturing, product prices, etc. In order to deal with such problems effectively, executives need information which enables them to see what effects individual conditions (such as, for example, a change in raw material prices) have had on costs.

While price and volume variances have been listed above as examples of items not controllable by operating management, there may be controllable elements in these variances. A few companies interviewed stated that price variances had a limited usefulness in evaluating purchasing activities. The following example cited by Paul C. Taylor is typical of others encountered in the field study.

"One company was purchasing a rubber grommet from an outside supplier. A standard purchase price of 32 cents per hundred had been established for it at a time when the company had just started to use a standard cost system. On the very first invoice received for the part, it was noted, when the standard price was entered on the invoice and extended by the quantity for later accounting purposes, that the billing price had jumped to 49 cents per hundred.

"Here is where control begins. It was determined that the immediate difference was caused by the fact that purchase orders had been placed for a quarter's supply of the part at a volume large enough to obtain the best price, but faulty shipping instructions had caused deliveries in small quantities at the higher billing price. Since little was involved in storing this part and since it involved relatively little money, it was possible to discontinue the policy of numerous releases against the purchase orders.

"This incident led to an investigation of the ordering of other small parts such as screws, nails, taper pins, rivets, cotter keys, etc., and oddly enough, it was found that often purchase orders for these highly standardized parts were being placed as frequently as twice a week. This, of course, resulted in a backbreaking load of duplicate motions and clerical effort to follow up, inspect, receive, store and record.[3]

Volume variances arise from non-standard utilization of production factors whose costs do not vary with volume. Causes of such variances may arise outside the company (e.g. unusually good or bad business conditions, inability to obtain materials) or they may reflect internal planning and supervision in use of productive facilities (e.g., poor planning and scheduling of work or a standard which is too easily attained). To initiate action called for by volume variance usually is a responsibility of management at the executive level. However, factual information as to the sources and causes of volume

---

[3] "Functioning of Standards in Cost Control," *N.A.A. Bulletin*, March 1951, pp. 796-7.

variances is needed in order that those responsible may know in which direction to turn.

The field study indicates that much remains to be done in practice with the problem of determining causes of and responsibility for volume variances. However, a few companies reported methods for assembling information useful in improving utilization of facilities within the factory. Among these were the following:

1. Special studies of scheduled versus actual machine hours had been made from time to time and temporary reports rendered during the course of the study. Action based upon the most recent study had raised average machine utilization from 60% to 80% of potential capacity. This company kept a continuous record of the ratio of man to machine hours. This record was stated to be highly useful in determining how much additional output could be obtained from machines by adding more men and also in securing the optimum balance between men and machines.

2. Cooperation between accountants and engineers in establishing causes and responsibility for idle machine time was stressed by another company. Here the accounting department accumulated idle time reported to each center under a classification of causes designated by the foremen. Staff engineers were then assigned to investigate underlying conditions and to suggest methods for improvement. In such investigations it was often necessary to trace causes beyond the cost center where the delay occurred and to take actions which were beyond the authority of the individual foreman who reported the idle time. For example, excessive machine downtime for set-up was traced to a combination of inaccurate stores records and faulty inspection in a prior process. Changeovers made when materials ran out before an order was completed and delays for adjustment needed because materials were not uniform resulted in low production.

3. The cost accountant for this company stated that records which permitted quick accumulation of number of hours machines were operated had helped management avoid unwise decisions. Here requests for additional equipment had been denied when these records showed that machines already in the plant were being used below their capacity.

The analysis of volume variances seems to offer opportunities to the accountant, for the field study shows it has had much less attention than have direct costs of material and labor. While the latter have undoubtedly been the more important components of total cost in some companies, increasing use of expensive equipment to achieve lower production costs makes it essential to control utilization of this equipment if the expected economies are to be realized.

8

## Administrative Decision Variances

Other variances for which responsibility rests with management at executive levels arise from administrative decisions authorizing deviations from standards. Such decisions are often reflected in costs as extra allowances or as variances caused by use of non-preferred equipment, overtime, etc. These variances may originate in actions to overcome difficulties such as shortage of material and labor, to compensate for obsolete standards until they can be revised, or to allow for alternatives not provided for in standards. While the variances usually constitute costs in excess of standard, they are not necessarily undesirable. For example, one company stated that unfavorable material yield variances often result from use of sub-standard grades of material, but that yield losses can be more than offset by a favorable price on the materials. At the same time, careful analysis is needed to show management when decisions to take advantage of opportunities to buy low priced materials will be profitable. It is also important to distinguish between yield variances due to processing efficiency (for which departmental supervisors are responsible) and yield variances ascribable to executive decisions to use different grades of material.

In summary with respect to analysis of variances by responsibility, a variance should measure success in control over cost factors assigned to a single responsibility. As expressed by Norman A. Coan:

> ". . . one of the fundamental rules of utilizing the technique of variances . . . is . . . 'keep them pure,' i.e., unmixed with each other and a corollary to the rule is to align variance determination to the organization and to assigned responsibilities."[4]

The first step in accomplishing this objective is to separate those cost factors which are directly controllable by operating supervision from the other factors for which executive management is responsible. Among the latter, there are some which can be controlled by executive decision and others which management cannot control. Nevertheless, top management needs to know what effect the noncontrollables have had on costs.

---

[4] "Variances Must Be Forged Into Familiar Tools," *N.A.A. Bulletin*, June 1950, pp. 1227-8.

# ANALYSIS OF VARIANCES
# BY CAUSES

Variances reflect the effect on costs which certain events or conditions have produced. Before management can decide whether or not action is called for and, if so, what should be done, it is necessary to know what caused the variance to arise. The analysis of variances by causes is therefore an important aspect of the use of standard costs to attain improved cost control.

However, the field studies show that in many companies using standard costs the accounting reports contain little information as to variance causes. One explanation of this fact seems to be that accountants are accustomed to the classification of costs by cost elements (i.e., material, labor, and overhead) for costing inventories and they follow the same classification in developing costs for operating cost control purposes. As a result, cost control reports display variances by items of cost rather than by cause. In commenting on this point, a writer has said:

> "In most standard cost systems accounting departments have approached the subject of variance accounts almost entirely from an accounting viewpoint instead of from an operating viewpoint. The result is that variances are created to which are attached "labels" that express accounting terminology. This terminology is almost without exception foreign to the executives and operators, and it is extremely difficult for them or anyone else to understand. Furthermore, variances by accounts, such as labor, repairs and maintenance, etc., are developed which express only the fact that there is a difference between the budget and actual but give no reason therefore."[5]

While the analysis of variances according to elements and items of cost is not without service to operating management, it seems probable that more emphasis upon variance causes can add usefulness to many standard cost systems.

## Who Determines Variance Causes?

Experience of the companies interviewed seems to show that the explana-

---

[5] Joseph B. Copper, "Accounting by Causes vs. Accounting by Accounts," *N.A.A. Bulletin*, December 15, 1945, p. 319.

tion and interpretation of variances is best developed through independent analysis made by the cost accountant working in close collaboration with operating supervisors. While interpretation of events in terms of variance causes is primarily a function of the operating supervisor or executive, the cost department collects and organizes statistical information relating to variance causes. By appropriate classification, the significance of the information can be brought out and through reports variance cause data is made accessible to management. In large companies, the analysis and control of variances may be assigned to one or more specialized departments. As an example, one company has a personnel efficiency department that devotes its entire time to the study of labor costs and analysis of labor variances. In other companies the work is often done by cost analysts attached to the cost accounting department but who, at the same time, are acquainted with and work as a team with production management. Where company size does not justify specialization, the function is performed by members of the regular cost accounting staff in cooperation with factory personnel.

## *Approaches to Analysis of Variances by Causes*

Practice shows two general approaches to the analysis of variances by causes. These are:

1. To determine variance causes by special studies which are made apart from the recurrent operations of accumulating and reporting costs.

2. To incorporate the analysis by cause into the cost accounting system by providing individual variance accounts for each of the principal causes for which a variance is to be isolated. Periodic reports giving variances classified by cause are then prepared directly from the accounts.

Under the first approach variances are accumulated in the accounts by responsibility and by cost element, but not by cause. The variances developed serve to raise questions which are then answered by additional investigation to determine causes of the variances which have arisen. Under the second approach, the system is designed to provide direct answers in terms of variance causes without further analysis.

The use of variance accounts for accumulating variances by causes adds to the clerical work required in accounting for costs, although the amount of additional work depends upon the number and complexity of the variance classifications employed. However, one company stated that the desired analysis by cause could actually be made more cheaply this way than by special study because the analysis was thereby reduced to routine operations which do not require skilled cost analysts.

11

# DEPARTMENTAL MANUFACTURING EFFICIENCY
## ON COMPLETED OPERATIONS

### ——— Plant

### Dept. No............................

| Code | REASON FOR VARIANCE | | MONTH OF | | | YEAR TO DATE | | |
|---|---|---|---|---|---|---|---|---|
| | | | ACTUAL HOURS | VARIANCE HOURS | COST | ACTUAL HOURS | VARIANCE HOURS | COST |
| 0—No reason, variances less than 10 per cent. | | C | | | | | | |
| 1—Estimated running time too high. Reported to Stds. Dep't. | | N | | | | | | |
| 2—Estimated set-up time too high. Reported to Stds. Dep't. | | N | | | | | | |
| 3—Men's effort and/or ability above average. | | C | | | | | | |
| 5—New machine, standard has not been changed. | | N | | | | | | |
| 6—Change in methods, standard has not been changed. | | N | | | | | | |
| 7—New or improved tools, standard has not been changed. | | N | | | | | | |
| 8—Used set-up from previous job. | | C | | | | | | |
| 9—Time set for man operating one machine. Ran two. | | C | | | | | | |
| 10—Time clock registers to 0.1 hour only. | | N | | | | | | |
| 11—Work done under special supervision. | | C | | | | | | |
| TOTAL GAINS | | | | | | | | |
| 0—No reason, variances less than 10 percent. | | C | | | | | | |
| 51—Standard too low. Reported to Standards Department. | | N | | | | | | |
| 52—First time job was made. | | C | | | | | | |
| 53—Slow or obsolete machine used. | | N | | | | | | |
| 54—Planning not correct. Was changed. Stds. Dep't. notified. | | N | | | | | | |
| 55—Could not follow oper. as planned, delivery requirements. | | N | | | | | | |
| 56—Operations in previous departments not performed as planned. | | C | | | | | | |
| 57—Time set for man operating two machines. One available. | | N | | | | | | |
| 58—Quantity too small. | | N | | | | | | |
| 59—Extra set-up result of machine break down. | | N | | | | | | |
| 60—Extra work. | | N | | | | | | |

(Continued on next page)

**EXHIBIT 1**

(Continued from preceding page)

## DEPARTMENTAL MANUFACTURING EFFICIENCY
## ON COMPLETED OPERATIONS

| Code | REASON FOR VARIANCE | | MONTH OF | | | YEAR TO DATE | | |
|------|---------------------|---|----------------|------------------|------|----------------|------------------|------|
| | | | ACTUAL HOURS | VARIANCE HOURS | COST | ACTUAL HOURS | VARIANCE HOURS | COST |
| 61—Two men had to be assigned to job due to nature of job. | | N | | | | | | |
| 62—Learner, apprentice, or student. | | N | | | | | | |
| 63—Man inexperienced. Undergoing instructions. | | N | | | | | | |
| 64—Different operators used due to difficulty of job. | | C | | | | | | |
| 65—Assisting inexperienced operator on another machine. | | N | | | | | | |
| 66—Man's effort and/or ability below average. | | C | | | | | | |
| 67—Oper. not performed correctly. Add'l time required. | | C | | | | | | |
| 68—Parts spoiled. Had to make additional parts. | | C | | | | | | |
| 69—Tools not available at time job was started. | | N | | | | | | |
| 70—Trying out new tools. | | N | | | | | | |
| 71—Tools not correct when job was started. Had to be corrected. | | N | | | | | | |
| 72—Broke tool. Time lost redressing and sharpening. | | C | | | | | | |
| 73—Oversized material used. | | N | | | | | | |
| 74—Castings warped, but are within Foundry tolerances | | N | | | | | | |
| 75—Castings not to dimensions. Time lost waiting for instructions. | | N | | | | | | |
| 76—Material too hard. Frequent sharpening of tools required. | | N | | | | | | |
| 77—Improper supervision. | | C | | | | | | |
| 79—Illegible Blue Prints. | | N | | | | | | |
| 80—Blowholes and porous castings. | | N | | | | | | |
| 81—Sheet stock—Secondary material or scrap ends used. | | N | | | | | | |
| 99—Full quantity or operations not complete. | | N | | | | | | |
| TOTAL LOSSES | | | | | | | | |
| TOTAL | | | | | | | | |
| EFFICIENCY % CONTROLLABLE BY FOREMAN | | C | | | | | | |
| EFFICIENCY % NON-CONTROLLABLE | | N | | | | | | |
| EFFICIENCY % OVERALL | | | | | | | | |

13

Repetitive analysis procedures require the use of a predetermined classification of variance causes. A system by itself does not have intelligence and hence the questions it is expected to answer and the responses it can give are limited to those provided for in designing the system. For this reason supplementary special studies are also needed from time to time to obtain information about variance causes which is not provided by the regular reports. Therefore, most companies use both approaches to some extent.

In designing a standard cost system, selection of the variances to be determined periodically is an important step. Some variances indicate opportunities for cost reduction while others measure the effect of management decisions to deviate from the established standards. Therefore each variance account provided in the chart of accounts is intended to collect information for a specific purpose. In general, the following criteria seem to be important in selecting the number and types of variances to be determined regularly.

1. The amount and relative importance of variances arising from a given cause.

2. Whether a given variance arises from recurrent or non-recurrent causes.

3. The need to separate variances which point to opportunities for cost reduction from other variances concerning which direct action cannot be taken.

Rather obviously the periodic isolation of a variance is useful only when the amount in question is sufficiently important. Moreover, the need to avoid too much detail in reporting to management acts as a limiting factor. For these reasons, variance causes of major importance in the control of costs are singled out for attention. As an example, a company which found it especially important to control raw material costs had established a series of variances to measure usage and yields in each manufacturing process. In contrast another company uses only a single over-all material cost variance account because material represents a comparatively small fraction of the total product cost and experience shows that losses of material are small.

On the other hand a variance which is too broad may fail to bring out important information about the working of individual causes in influencing costs. An illustration of this is provided by the analyses of direct labor variances shown on a single production time ticket. This ticket showed an

14

overall variance of only \$0.12. However, when this ticket was analyzed to ascertain causes of the variance, the following results were obtained:

| Cause of Variance | Amounts | |
|---|---|---|
| | Favorable | Unfavorable |
| 1. Rate of pay | \$2.74 | |
| 2. Size of crew | —— | |
| 3. Extra set-ups | 1.18 | |
| 4. Use of non-standard equipment | 1.24 | |
| 5. Operator efficiency | —— | \$5.28 |
| | \$5.16 | \$5.28 |

It was stated that management definitely should know about the efficiency variance in this case. In order to provide this information, the company makes a daily analysis of direct labor variance by causes listed above. Daily computation of the variances is feasible because they are obtained from data which the company finds essential in recording production and accounting for variances and inventory costs on a monthly basis.[6]

## Examples of Variance Analysis by Cause

In practice, procedures followed in analyzing variances by cause differ widely from company to company. These differences in procedure are explained by differences in manufacturing processes employed and by differing managerial preferences as to the amount and kind of information wanted. In order to illustrate the analysis of variances by cause, the following examples have been selected from practices of companies interviewed.

### Example 1: Analysis of Direct Labor Variances

This company's operations consist of machining and assembly on a job order basis. The number of employees in all operations is approximately 3800. Labor variances, expressed in man-hours only, are analyzed according to a predetermined list of causes.

On completion of each operation, the foreman indicates the reason for labor hours over or under standard, using the code shown in Exhibit 1. Timekeepers record the information on time cards and summaries are produced by mechanical tabulation. When the variance is less than 10% of standard time, no explanation is required. If a given variance is due

---

[6] For an illustration of the daily development of such variances as a comparatively simple and inexpensive clerical function, see Norman A. Coan, "Two Compact Forms for the Measurement of Operating Performance Under Standard Costs," *N.A.A. Bulletin*, September 1949, pp. 37-42.

## DIRECT LABOR PERFORMANCE

**(Left hand side of report)**

Department............................................................ Month of............................................................

| Product LINE | ACTUAL | ALLOWED | VARIANCE | COST RATIO ALLOWED TO STANDARD | STANDARD | TOTAL NON-STANDARD |
|---|---|---|---|---|---|---|
| A | $179 | $156 | $23 | 130% | $120 | $59 |
| B | 200 | 215 | 15* | 110 | 195 | 5 |
| Totals | | | | | | |

## CAUSES OF NON-STANDARD

**(Right hand side of report)**

| TO MAINTAIN LABOR STANDARDS | | | | | | | TO MAINTAIN QUALITY STANDARDS | | | |
|---|---|---|---|---|---|---|---|---|---|---|
| | 1 | 2 | 3 | 4 | 5 | 6A | | 6B | | |
| Sub-total | Day Work | Wage Protection | Std. to Piece Rate | Change in Piece Rate | Auth. Method Change | Opn. not in Std. Cost | Sub-total | Opn. not in Std. Cost | | |
| $19 | $10 | | | | $10* | $19 | $40 | $40 | | |
| 0 | | | 7* | | 7 | | 5 | | 5 | |
| Totals | | | | | | | | | | |

* Favorable.

**EXHIBIT 2**

to two or more causes, the foreman apportions the variance hours between the causes. Variance data recorded by the timekeepers is summarized monthly by the accounting department to produce the report shown in Exhibit 1. In the report, individual variance causes are designated as controllable or noncontrollable according to whether or not the cause is controllable by the foremen. This classification of variances was developed jointly by accounting and top factory management. While the position of some items may be questionable, the classification is sufficiently reliable to have practical usefulness. Supervision over foremen is relied upon to overcome any tendency to designate controllable causes as non-controllable.

It was stated that supplementary explanations are seldom needed since the reports have been designed to answer most of the questions which arise in connection with labor variance causes.

## Example 2: Analysis of Direct Labor Variances

This company's manufacturing operations are characterized by numerous alternative processing methods and sequences. Exacting product quality standards also make necessary a large volume of reworking operations. Managerial efforts to control costs are directed more toward attaining products of the desired quality at the desired costs than they are toward complete standardization of production processes. In order that production executives may have information needed to exercise this control, the following monthly analysis of direct labor variances is made. The company has approximately 1600 employees in all operations and annual sales of $18 million.

The first step in its analysis of direct labor variances is a monthly comparison between actual direct labor cost and allowed direct labor cost by product lines. Figures resulting from this comparison are reported in the initial columns of the form shown as Exhibit 2. Allowed cost includes standard operations and a normal amount of non-standard operations. Foremen are responsible for variances from allowed cost and this comparison serves to show what effect these variances have had on costs of products manufactured. The report illustrated is prepared for executive management and reports of a different type are used in reporting variances to foremen which analyze all non-standard costs.

The second step in this analysis is a comparison between actual direct labor cost and standard direct labor cost. Variances which result show how close actual product costs have been to standard product costs.

By a third step in the analysis, the variances from standard direct labor cost are broken down by cause, as shown in the right hand portion of Exhibit 2. It will be noted that the variance causes are divided into two types, viz., (1) variances incurred to maintain labor standards and (2) variances incurred to maintain quality standards. Each of these types is then exemplified by such causes as operation on day work instead of piece work, authorized method changes and changes in piece rates. Variances, to maintain quality standards, arise from a variety of causes dependent upon the department in which the non-standard operations are performed. Hence the causes reported on the form are not pre-listed.

## Example 3: Analysis of Direct Material Variances

Inasmuch as direct materials constitute approximately 80% of manufacturing cost for this company, the company has placed major emphasis

17

upon control and reduction of direct material cost. The stated objective was to provide a simple and flexible program for investigating causes of material losses and to stimulate action to reduce costs. In contrast with the foregoing examples, repetitive analysis following a predetermined pattern has been avoided.

Quantity variances for direct materials are available by departments with breakdowns by kind of materials used. This makes possible for the chief cost accountant to detect and localize major variances. Analyses of these variances are made by a staff of three cost analysts permanently assigned to such studies. On assignment to a project, one of these men goes into the department concerned and studies the usage of the materials in question under actual operating conditions. An individual study may cover a period of weeks or longer and may entail a balancing of materials coming in against materials going out. Accounting for materials going out includes determining the quantities of good material in products, scrap, waste, and all other possible dispositions of material until causes of the variances are discovered.

The staff cost analyst then makes an informal report of his findings to the chief cost accountant and the latter takes the matter up with the production supervisor concerned to devise possible remedial actions. Production men have been trained to work with the cost department through company policy which emphasizes team work and oral communication. It was stated that savings directly traceable to cost analysis amply repay the costs of the analysis work.

*Example 4: Analysis of Controllable Overhead*

The fact that the number of actual labor hours paid for differs from the number of standard labor hours allowed for a given period tends to cause a controllable overhead variance as well as a direct labor variance. The overhead variance arises because those overhead expenses which vary with the number of hours worked are increased by excess hours. In order to emphasize the fact that efforts to control the latter portion of the overhead variance must be directed at the excess hours, this company shows among the controllable charges of each department a variance entitled "Overhead Gain or Loss Due to Direct Labor Variance." After separation of this item, the remaining controllable overhead variance is ascribable to non-standard rates of usage in variable overhead rates.

The following hypothetical data illustrate the company's method of calculating overhead usage control figures.

18

| | Budget Allowance for Month | | | | |
|---|---|---|---|---|---|
| | Variable per direct labor dollar | Total Variable | Fixed | Total Allowed | Actual Expense | Variance |
| Direct Labor | | | | $1300 | $1376 | ($76) |
| Overhead expenses | $0.60 | $826 | $825 | $1651 | $1790 | ($139) |
| Overhead loss due to excess direct labor* | | | | (46) | | (46) |
| Expense controllable by departmental superintendent | | | | $1605 | $1790 | ($185) |

\* Excess direct labor times variable overhead ratio
$76 times $0.60 = $45.60 or $46.

## Example 5: *Analysis of All Manufacturing Cost Variances*

One of the large companies interviewed prepares a monthly analysis report covering all causes of cost variances arising from manufacturing operations in the plant called upon by the interviewer. The classification of variance causes is designed to bring out information of interest to top management at the plant. A list of these causes together with an indication of the content of each class is given below. The order is that in which variance causes are listed on the company's report.

A. Usual items (e.g., increased cost of transportation incurred to obtain raw materials needed to maintain plant output during period of unusually high production.)

B. Price and wage levels
(Items listed in detail with subdivisions for purchases from standard and off-standard sources.)

C. Volume or fixed expense absorption
(General plant overhead shown separately from other plant fixed costs. Both are subdivided to break out significant causes contributing to volume variance—e.g., labor crew inflexibility, allowances for major repairs, vacation allowances, etc.)

D. Noncurrent standards
(Variances due to changes in operation standards not yet carried through to product cost standards.)

E. Product and facility mix
(Variances due to off-standard use of facilities, off-standard sources of services used.)

F. Material substitution and mix
(In detail by items.)

19

G. Material usage variances
   (In detail by materials.)

H. Direct labor performance
   (Listed by plant divisions.)

I. All other variances
   (Variances of miscellaneous nature not otherwise classified above.)

*Example 6: Organization for Analysis of Variances*

This company provides a particularly interesting illustration because of its intensive development of variance analysis and because it utilizes a combination of periodic reports and special studies to bring out variance causes. The company had used standard costs for a number of years and had provided management with reports which classified current variances by responsibilities and by the principal causes. A review of the company's variance reports indicated that actual costs experienced were reasonably close to standard costs. However, further investigation of the existing variance reporting plan brought out the following opportunities for improvement through more intensive analysis of variances:

1. Unfavorable variances were largely offset by favorable variances within the same classification and accordingly did not appear significant in variance reports. This indicated that cost reductions could be made if these individual variances were brought to managements' attention.

2. Many variances seemed insignificant when viewed in relation to total costs incurred in an individual period. Nevertheless, some of these variances were recurrent and indicated worthwhile opportunities for cost reduction when accumulated over a longer span of time.

3. Management sometimes needed more detailed information in order to take corrective action. Since many situations were nonrecurrent, this information could not be included in routine reports, but would have to be prepared when needed.

The company then decided to establish a continuing detailed analysis of operating variances. In doing this, two important questions arose, namely, (1) how to organize the work in order to insure its being done properly and (2) how to provide for communication of the results to operating management in a manner which would enable the company to realize benefits from the analysis.

A cost analyst was already attached to the works auditor's staff at each plant, but the time of this analyst was largely taken up with routine duties in preparing monthly variance reports. It was decided that analytical study of the type desired would be most effective if unhampered by functions which had to be performed on a time schedule. Moreover, it was necessary to provide adequately for the communication of results to operating management in a manner which would insure its full participation. In order to accomplish these results the analytical accounting functions at each plant were classified in three separate groups, viz.

1. General functions, consisting of repetitive operations such as preparation of monthly cost and variance reports.

2. Special cost variance analysis functions, consisting of intensive studies of cost variances in selected departments and collaboration with operating and industrial engineering personnel to develop methods for reducing costs and improving cost controls.

3. Special sales order analysis functions, consisting of studies of cost-sales price relationships to provide management with information useful in selling and pricing.

The resulting organization for the works accounting division is shown below.

*Organization Chart of Works Accounting Section*

Works Auditor

Assistant Works Auditor

| General Functions | Variance Analysis Functions | Order Analysis Functions |
|---|---|---|
| Works Cost Analyst | Variance Analyst | Order Cost Analyst |

Functions of the cost analysis section are stated as follows:

1. To make intensive analysis of cost variances within selected departments and to collaborate with operating and industrial engineering personnel to develop recommendations for reductions in each element of cost.

2. To establish or revise cost controls as a result of cost variance studies.

21

3. To establish and maintain measurement of results for each variance analysis project presented to management.

4. To maintain close follow-up of results of corrective action on each project and to present auxiliary studiés of remaining unfavorable variance causes as required.

5. To report deviations from established accounting procedures and cost principles as disclosed by intensive analysis.

Study of variances with the thoroughness contemplated made it necessary to concentrate the analysis work on selected projects. Once a specific cost has been chosen for intensive analysis, all aspects of the problem are studied to find the factors which influence the cost and to find methods for both improving control and reducing costs. After the initial investigation, the project is followed as long as seems desirable in order to gain the benefits of accumulated experience and to measure progress. Monthly operating reports to management include a section summarizing progress in the variance analysis projects under way. This information is presented under the following headings:

### Progress in Variance Analysis Program

| Project Title | Current Month's Variance | Improvement over Base Period | | Number of Months Measured |
| --- | --- | --- | --- | --- |
| | | This Month | To Date | |
| xx | xx | xx | xx | xx |
| xx | xx | xx | xx | xx |

In discussing the program, company representatives stressed the following points: (1) that variance analysis is a service to operating supervisors which gives them information they can use to control and reduce costs, (2) that variance analysis is an accounting function, (3) that competent personnel must be available for the analytical works, and (4) that fairly substantial expenditures must be made to carry on the program. With respect to the last point, it was stated that measured savings had justified expenditures made.

In contrast with the above examples, it seems that some companies do not fully realize the potential benefits from their standard cost systems because they have not provided the analysis needed to develope the significance of variance data and the means for effective communication of such information to operating management. These two aspects must, of course, go together, for analysis is obviously without point unless the results are put to use. While the company whose methods are described in the last example above is a large one, its manufacturing cost accounting operations are decentralized with

22

a variance analysis section at each plant. The plant in which operation of the variance analysis program was observed by the interviewer has approximately 2900 hourly employees. Successful operation of the same variance analysis program was reported by the company in a plant having 550 employees. At the latter location it was not found necessary to establish a new analytical section in the organization. Analyses have also been made in individual departments having as few as three employees. Hence, the same methods would appear to be as serviceable to a small company having only one plant as they are in individual plants of a large company.

# REPORTING VARIANCES
# TO MANAGEMENT

The end product of variance analysis ordinarily appears in the form of reports which are prepared to convey to management the information developed by analysis. These reports are primarily control reports rather than financial reports, although combination of control and financial aspects is sometimes made in reporting to top management.

All of the companies interviewed which use standard costs for cost control purposes have formal reports to summarize variances by responsibilities and by cost elements. However, information as to variance causes is often communicated orally or through informal memoranda prepared in response to specific requests. On the other hand, some companies have designed their variance reports to bring out variances in terms of causes significant to management at various levels in the organization.

*Summary Control Reports for Executive Management*

Since top management cannot be familiar with all operating details, reports summarize variances from standards periodically. Executives characteristically rely upon checking performance at certain key control points. For this reason, the information presented in variance reports should aid the executive in appraising the effectiveness with which the organization has functioned during the period covered by the report. Moreover, the reports should, if possible, shed light upon the principal problems with which top management is concerned. All of this needs to be done in terms familiar to the executive concerned rather than in a form which implies familiarity with accounting techniques.

The field study showed that variances are usually reported to top management monthly. In addition to monthly reports, executives at middle levels (e.g., the plant manager) often receive weekly and daily summaries of variances for direct labor, direct materials, and any other costs for which frequent checks on control are desired. Case examples of the use of summary control reports by three companies are given below.

*Example 1:* This company, which has emphasized decentralization of manufacturing operations and diversification of products, found the classification of variances to be an important matter for top management control. A top-level monthly variance report is prepared which appears as follows:

*Manufacturing Variance from Standard Cost*

| | Variances | | | Total | | Std. Mfg. Cost | % Variance to Std. |
|---|---|---|---|---|---|---|---|
| | Operating | Price | Volume | Actual | Budget | | |
| *Division A* | | | | | | | |
| Plant 1 | xx | xx | xx | xx | xx | xx | xx |
| etc. | | | | | | | |
| | | | | | | | |
| *Division B* | | | | | | | |
| Plant 1 | xx | xx | xx | xx | xx | xx | xx |
| etc. | xx | xx | xx | xx | xx | xx | xx |

The operating classification includes direct material quantity, direct labor performance, and controllable overhead variances. Division management is held responsible for these variances. Price variance covers variances from standard direct material prices and standard direct labor rates. These are viewed as the result of outside market conditions. Volume variance, arising from under or overabsorption of fixed burden, is considered by this company to be a top management responsibility.

*Example 2:* A somewhat different classification of variances is employed here in a monthly report prepared primarily for the manager in charge of each plant. This report includes a comparative summary of cost variances classified under the following headings.[7]

> Variances subject to cost reduction
> > By departmental supervisors
> > By top management
>
> Variances resulting from volume of business
> Variances resulting from company policy
> Variances resulting from miscellaneous causes

In commenting on this statement, it was stated that:

> ". . . the first thing the management wants to know is the *variances which are subject to cost reduction.* This should be the first item shown in an analysis of variances. This is the item which they must do something about. Therefore, this should be emphasized at all times, whether the results are being presented to a chief executive, general superintendent, or departmental superintendent.

[7] From Joseph B. Copper, "Accounting by Causes vs. Accounting by Accounts," *N.A.A. Bulletin,* December 15, 1945.

"Management is next interested in the *variances created by operating level.* This is not an item that is of interest to the departmental superintendents or to general superintendents but is of great interest to the chief executive. . .

"The next class of variances in which management is vitally interested is *variances created by company policy.* These are the variances that are created by policies laid down with respect to amortization, accelerated depreciation, obsolescence, contingencies, etc. . . . .

"The last section would be *miscellaneous variances*—items having to do a great deal with straight accounting, such as inventory adjustments, revision of budget standards, pension payments, etc. Generally, these variances in total should net a relatively small figure."

## DEPARTMENTAL MANUFACTURING EFFICIENCY ON OPERATIONS COMPLETED

### Week Ending April 29, 1951 and Year to Date

| | THIS WEEK | | | | | YEAR TO DATE | | |
| | | | Efficiency % | | | | | |
| DEPARTMENT | Non-Sd. Hours | Actual Hours on Std. | Variance from Std. Hours | On Total | Controllable by Foreman | Variance from Std. Hours | Total | Controllable by Foreman |
|---|---|---|---|---|---|---|---|---|
| **MACHINING** | | | | | | | | |
| 12 Blacksmith | | | | | | | | |
| 21 Auto. Screw Mach. | | | | | | | | |
| 22 Lathe | | | | | | | | |
| 24 Screw Mach. | | | | | | | | |
| Total Machining | | | | | | | | |
| **ASSEMBLY** | | | | | | | | |
| 23 Inspection | | | | | | | | |
| 29 Painting | | | | | | | | |
| 43 Assembly | | | | | | | | |
| 46 " | | | | | | | | |
| 48 " Electrical | | | | | | | | |
| Total Assembly | | | | | | | | |
| Grand Total | | | | | | | | |

## EXHIBIT 3

*Example 3:* A weekly summary of direct labor variances to inform top management as to performance of departments and machine centers is shown in Exhibit 3. Similar summaries by jobs and by product lines are available. Supporting these summaries is a detailed breakdown of variances by cause (illustrated in Exhibit 1). Together, these reports are intended to present the variances in sufficient detail to make them practi-

26

cally self explanatory. In this company variance reports are separate from the financial statements. It was stated that this separation has been made to attract the attention of management to conditions requiring specific action.

While the terminology employed differs from company to company, it is evident that variance reports for top management commonly recognize three basic variance causes, viz:

1. Operating causes, such as quantity of materials used, labor performance, etc.
2. Prices paid for cost factors.
3. Volume

The operating category consists largely of variances over which a substantial degree of control can be exercised and hence it measures operating effectiveness of the organization. On the other hand, the price and volume categories reflect the effect which these two external factors have had on the company's costs.

## Reporting Variances to Factory Supervisors

Responsibility for directing manufacturing activities rests upon line management directly in charge of operations, although various staff specialists are provided to assist operating management in its work. The cost accounting department stands in the latter position in the organization, for one of its functions is to provide information which is useful in directing operations.

However, provision of information is not enough, for it must be actually used. This point was expressed in the following words by a speaker at an N.A.A. Cost Conference:

> "We also recognize that we cannot achieve economical operation by sitting at a desk and devising systems, unless we secure the intelligent cooperation of the people in our organization who spend the money. These people are our foremen. Through the process of education, we have tried to develop in our foremen a cost consciousness which emphasizes the importance of getting full value for every dollar spent."[8]

Discussion with company representatives in the course of the field study indicated that strong backing from top management is the first essential in effective operation of standard costs for cost control. Given such backing, a program of education can be utilized to develop among supervisors and foremen the desired attitude of cost consciousness and skill in using standards and variances as tools with which to control costs. At the same time, the cost accounting department must be conducted as a service to operating men.

---

[8] Nicholas St. Peter, "How Our Profit Planning Program Works—A Case Study," *N.A.A. Conference Proceedings*, 1949, pp. 83-84.

The information supplied to departmental supervisors usually takes the form of current cost control reports which tell the individual supervisor how his performance compares with standards. In addition to showing what variances have occurred, these reports need to point out the sources of the variances and to do this promptly in order that action may be taken before the opportunity has passed. Exhibit 4 illustrates the form in which cost reports are prepared for foremen by one organization contributing material for this study.

## COST CENTER ANALYSIS
### FACTORY

| VARIANCES | | | ACCOUNT | ACTUAL YEAR TO DATE | THIS PERIOD | | | |
|---|---|---|---|---|---|---|---|---|
| THIS PERIOD | YEAR TO DATE | 99 | | | EXT. BUDG. ALLOW. | CURRENT ALLOW. | ACTUAL | |
| | | 01 | DIRECT LABOR | | | | | |
| | | | **TOTAL DIR. LABOR** | | | | | |
| | | 11 | SUPERVISION | | | | | |
| | | 14 | OVERTIME EXCESS | | | | | |
| | | 15 | INDIRECT LABOR | | | | | |
| | | | **TOTAL IND. LABOR** | | | | | |
| | | 22 | GENERAL SUPPLIES | | | | | |
| | | 23 | JIGS, TOOLS & FIX. | | | | | |
| | | 151 | JIGS, T. & FIX. - LABOR | | | | | |
| | | 24 | FUEL | | | | | |
| | | 30 | PURCHASED POWER | | | | | |
| | | 31 | WATER | | | | | |
| | | 41 | REPAIRS LAND & BLDG. | | | | | |
| | | 152 | REPAIRS L. & B. - LAB. | | | | | |
| | | 42 | REPAIRS M. & EQUIP. | | | | | |
| | | 153 | REP. M. & E. - LABOR | | | | | |
| | | 51 | SOC. SECURITY TAX | | | | | |
| | | 52 | | | | | | |
| | | 53 | | | | | | |
| | | 54 | | | | | | |
| | | 55 | VACATION ALLOWANCE | | | | | |
| | | 68 | NEW METHODS EXP. | | | | | |
| | | 69 | SPOILAGE | | | | | |
| | | | **DEPT. TOTAL** | | | | | |

**COMMENTS**

| ACTIVITY (VOLUME) | PRODUCTION | STANDARD | EFY. RATIO | T. C. RATIO | |
|---|---|---|---|---|---|
| ← CURRENT → | | | | | |
| ← Y. T. D. → | | | | | |

| PERIOD | RECOVERY | THIS PERIOD | YEAR TO DATE |
|---|---|---|---|
| STANDARD BUDGETED RECOVERY | | | |
| RECOVERY @ INDICATED ACTIVITY | | | |
| COST CENTER | KEYMAN | | |

CCAF

**EXHIBIT 4**

28

In reporting variances to management at the supervisory level, emphasis is placed upon cost factors directly controllable by the individual supervisor. Many companies exclude from cost and variance reports to supervisors all items for which the supervisor receiving the report is not directly responsible. Other companies include non-controllable items in current control reports as a matter of information or because there may be some contributory responsibility. As an example of the latter, one company which includes costs of depreciation, property taxes and insurance in departmental cost reports stated that it does so because it wants the foreman to be aware of the importance of such costs and of the effect which requests for additional equipment have on total costs of his department.

## Coordination of Reports

Discussion by the Committee on Research stressed two major points which need to be considered in developing a plan for reporting variances to management. These are:

1. Variance information must be timely.
2. Reports must provide the amount of detail needed at each level of management.

The manner in which these aims are achieved through use of carefully coordinated reports is illustrated by the following case example.

This company has daily control reports which build up to monthly summaries. In this manner, information prepared from day-to-day operations is used to compile monthly figures for variance control. Standards in the form of allowed hours for the attained production level constitute the basis for control and variances are measured from these standards. The allowed hour standards are developed primarily from past experience modified for known correctible conditions and by elimination of ineffective operations. Stress is placed upon gaining acceptance of the standards by the factory operators.

Actual production performance is reported at the end of each day on a daily production report (Exhibit 5).[9] In this report, "chargeable hours" are productive time charged directly to product cost at the standard cost per hour. "Non-chargeable hours" are non-productive time included as burden in the standard cost per chargeable hour. Both classes are measured against an allowed hour standard for control purposes.

The cost department at each plant completes the daily report by entering allowed hours and variances and a copy is sent to the responsible foreman the following morning. The foreman can then spot the exceptional variances and is usually in a position to take any indicated re-

[9] Figures shown in exhibits are hypothetical.

29

DAILY PRODUCTION REPORT

FINISHING DEPARTMENT

SAN FRANCISCO DIVISION          DATE 2-29-52

| DESCRIPTION | MACH. | SHIFT | NO. ON | AVGE PER HR | | | CHARGEABLE HOURS | | | | | | NON-CHARGEABLE HOURS | | | | | |
|---|---|---|---|---|---|---|---|---|---|---|---|---|---|---|---|---|---|---|
| | | | | ALL'D | ACT | | MAKE READY | | | RUN | | | SCHEDULED | | | UNSCHEDULED | | |
| | | | | | | | ALL'D | ACT | L/G | ALL'D | ACT | L/G | ALL'D | ACT | L/G | ALL'D | ACT | L/G |
| MILK CTN CARRIERS 7¼ x 2⅝ | | 1 | | ACT | 1776 | | | | | 6.5 | | | | | | | | |
| WEC | | | | | | | | | | | | | 1.0 | 1.0 | | | | |
| Total | | 1 | | ACT | 1775 | | | | | 6.5 | | | | 1.0 | 1.0 | — | | |
| 1ˢᵗ CRAX - 12¼ x 29¾ | | 1 | | 18000 | 15000 | | | | | 4.6 | | | | | | | | |
| 2ⁿᵈ BBV BAKER - 17¾ x 86⅜ | | 1 | | 5760 | 3600 | | | .7 | | .3 | | | | .3 | .3 | | | |
| — | | 2 | | — | 3400 | | | | | 2.2 | | | | .2 | .3 | | | |
| WEC | | 2 | | | | | | | | | | | | 1.5 | 2.0 | -.5 | | |
| Total | | 1 | | 10480 | 9076 | | | .7 | | 7.1 | | | | 2.1 | 2.6 | -.5 | .1 | .1 |
| Shift Total | % all'd | 1 | | | | | | | | | | | | | | | | |
| " " | " " | 2 | | | | | | | | | | | | | 87 % | | 41 % | |
| " " | L " | 3 | | | | | | | | | | | | | | | | |
| Total OC-48 | 92 " " | | | 6800 | 5825 | | | .7 | | 13.6 | | | | 2.1 | 3.6 | -.5 | .1 | .1 |
| Month to Date | 107 " " | | | | 60610 | | | 6.3.3 | | 127.1 | | | | 32.1 | 37.1 | -5.0 | 2.5 | 2.5 |

**EXHIBIT 5**

medial action while the order is still flowing through his department. From these departmental reports a daily summary is prepared and submitted to the plant manager and his superintendents. As these reports are reviewed each day, significant variances are checked and appropriate explanations are noted by a cost analyst working in collaboration with the responsible foreman. This routine brings exceptional items to light when they arise and therefore eliminates surprises at the end of the month. Factual information for later use in the monthly reports is also accumulated.

At the end of the month a departmental cost statement (Exhibit 6) provides a summary for the plant management. In addition, the report serves to inform the superintendent of each department as to costs and variances for which he is responsible. The sub-heading, "Total Controllable Costs," indicates where the superintendent's responsibility ends.

The lower sections of the report provide break-downs of material costs by type of material and of labor costs by machine or handwork cost centers. In the latter, budget hours represent the anticipated average volume of operation upon which the standard costs per hour are predicated at the time the annual manufacturing cost budget was prepared. They are displayed on this statement to furnish a comparison with actual volume of operation. Allowed hours represent the standard time allow-

30

Department  CARTON DEPARTMENT

| CURRENT MONTH | | | ITEMS OF COST | YEAR TO DATE | | COST PER | |
|---|---|---|---|---|---|---|---|
| VARIATION FROM STANDARD | ACTUAL | | | ACTUAL | VARIATION FROM STANDARD | CURRENT MONTH | YEAR TO DATE |
| (871) | 43,471 | 01 | Direct Labor Hourly | 386,305 | (703) | | |
| (2,174) | 10,052 | 02 | Indirect Labor Hourly | 70,606 | (2,257) | | |
| 2,489 | 304 | 04 | Overtime Penalty | 2,719 | (5) | | |
| (524) | 6,110 | 49 | Payroll Expense | 48,563 | (929) | | |
| (2,054) | | | Allowed Hour Variation—Labor Cost | | (36,338) | | |
| (3,134) | 59,937 | | Sub-Total—Labor Cost | 508,193 | (40,232) | | |
| (2,897) | 6,932 | 15 | Repairs Material | 38,447 | (5,450) | | |
| (688) | 2,662 | 16 | Misc. Supplies & Expense | 17,576 | (2,155) | | |
| (852) | 2,405 | 24 | Major Repairs Material | 15,897 | (3,833) | | |
| (1,489) | 6,856 | 60 | Maintenance Service | 48,352 | (4,174) | | |
| | | 62 | Steam Power | | | | |
| (23) | 188 | 63 | Electric Power | 1,473 | (77) | | |
| (58) | 4,527 | 64 | Gen. Mfg. Expense | 36,892 | (600) | | |
| (711) | | | Allowed Hour Variation—Other Cost | | (17,413) | | |
| (9,852) | 83,507 | | Total Controllable Cost | 666,830 | (73,934) | | |
| (5,324) | 22,498 | 65 | Fixed Costs | 151,730 | (7,604) | | |
| (15,176) | 106,005 | | Total Conversion Cost | 818,560 | (81,538) | | |
| 185 | 161,845 | 95 | Material Cost (See Below) | 1,321,571 | (1,469) | | |
| (14,991) | 267,850 | | TOTAL MANUFACTURING COST | 2,140,131 | (83,007) | | |
| | | | Units Produced | | | x x x x | x x x x |

| MATERIAL COST (CURRENT MONTH) | UNITS USED ( ) | | ACTUAL PRICE | MATERIAL COST STANDARD | MATERIAL USAGE VARIANCE |
|---|---|---|---|---|---|
| | ACTUAL | VARIATION FROM STD. | | | |
| Chip Boards | 1,049.883 | | 41.77 | 43,848 | |
| Manila Lined Boards | 264.019 | | 56.40 | 14,891 | |
| Patent Coated Boards | 241.757 | | 74.48 | 18,453 | |
| Other Boards | 612.607 | | 92.96 | 56,951 | |
| Egg Fillers | | | | 2,583 | |
| Misc. & Finishing Material | | | | 25,304 | 185 |
| Total Material Cost | 2,174.266 | | | 162,030 | 185 |

| CODE NO. | COST CENTER | BUDGET HOURS | ACTUAL HOURS | ALLOWED HOURS | LABOR COST BUD. RATE | ALLOWED HOUR VARIATION LABOR | % OF ALLOWED |
|---|---|---|---|---|---|---|---|
| 03 | Composing | 113.9 | 75.5 | 75.5 | 4.08 | | |
| 04 | Winding | 503.4 | 330.0 | 334.4 | 1.61 | 7 | 101.3 |
| 05 | Reoperation | 1,992.9 | 1,791.5 | 847.5 | 1.52 | (1,429) | (47.3) |
| 06 | Handwork | 1,803.1 | 1,646.7 | 1,507.6 | 1.58 | (219) | (91.6) |
| 07 | Die Making | 877.2 | 672.5 | 680.4 | 2.34 | 18 | 101.2 |
| 08 | Stripping | 4,839.0 | 3,062.5 | 3,097.7 | 2.03 | 71 | 101.1 |
| 09 | Finishing | 2,856.2 | 2,636.0 | 2,309.7 | 1.86 | (607) | (97.6) |
| 49 | Swift Food Pail Machine | 250.2 | 145.1 | 121.9 | 2.13 | (50) | (84.0) |
| 50 | Brightwood Gluers | 1,568.7 | 247.2 | 243.5 | 2.19 | (8) | (98.5) |
| 51 | Cu-Pak Egg Machine | 643.1 | | | 2.26 | | |
| 55 | Cello Gluer | 280.8 | 295.9 | 294.1 | 3.63 | (6) | (99.4) |
| 61 | Quart I.C. Pail Machine | 278.5 | 153.0 | 149.6 | 3.68 | (13) | (97.8) |
| | TOTAL | 28,816.8 | 20,555.4 | 19,126.0 | | (2,054) | (96.3) |

( ) Denotes Red Figure

## EXHIBIT 6

ance for the actual work performed during the period. The allowed hour variance represents the difference between actual and allowed hours extended by the labor portion of the standard cost per hour.

A summary of all operating variances is prepared in the form shown in Exhibit 7. This provides the plant manager with a picture of the operations of his entire plant. Furthermore, this statement serves as medium by which the home executive office receives an analysis of each plant's operating variances with appropriate explanations.

The reports described above serve to inform management at three

## Analysis of Operating Cost Variances
### (CURRENT MONTH)

| NO. | OPERATING DEPARTMENTS | DIRECT LABOR BUDGET VARIANCES | | | | | INDIRECT LABOR VARIANCE | OVERTIME PENALTY | PAYROLL EXPENSES | TOTAL LABOR VARIANCE | OTHER CONTROLLABLE | | TOTAL OPERATING VARIANCES |
| --- | --- | --- | --- | --- | --- | --- | --- | --- | --- | --- | --- | --- | --- |
| | | MISC. | NON-PRO-DUCTIVE | PREMIUM EXCESS | RETRO PAY | ALLOWED HOUR VARIANCE | | | | | ALLOWED HOUR | OTHER | |
| 10 | Raw Mat'l, Hdlg. & Stg. | 537 | | 237 | | | 120 | 42 | 11 | 1,007 | | 1,344 | 2,351 |
| 15 | Beaters & Jordans | 38 | (2) | | | | 64 | 344 | (113) | 333 | 3,205 | (975) | (642) |
| 16 | No. 1 Board Machine | 46 | 110 | | | | (195) | 34 | (38) | (215) | 2,086 | (591) | 2,399 |
| 17 | No. 2 Board Machine | (195) | 66 | 4 | | | (200) | (98) | (83) | (475) | 641 | (990) | 631 |
| 18 | No. 3 Board Machine | (134) | (71) | (17) | | | (65) | 68 | 95 | (353) | 39 | 1,958 | 2,146 |
| 20 | Sheet Liner | (14) | | 14 | | | | 51 | 11 | (41) | | 10 | 8 |
| 22 | Boardmill Finishing | 427 | | 22 | | | 81 | 224 | 56 | 771 | | 371 | 1,142 |
| 23 | Corr. Waste Baler | (45) | | | | | | 62 | (4) | 27 | | 200 | 227 |
| 24 | Carton Waste Baler | (40) | | | | | | 38 | (3) | 17 | | 226 | 243 |
| 34 | Paste Making | 11 | | | | | | 12 | (2) | 21 | | (7) | 14 |
| 36 | Paster | (69) | 52 | 3 | | | | 20 | (11) | (5) | | 1,512 | 1,505 |
| 37 | Corrugators | (2) | (191) | (688) | | | (226) | 433 | (146) | (820) | 3,147 | (949) | 1,378 |
| 39 | Corrugated Case | (179) | (197) | 98 | | | (951) | 724 | (364) | (1,238) | | (972) | (2,210) |
| 40 | Laminator | (1) | (17) | (2) | (969) | | (98) | 34 | (15) | (99) | | (125) | (224) |
| 41 | Carton | 665 | (787) | (365) | (384) | (2,054) | (2,174) | 2,489 | (524) | (3,134) | (711) | (6,007) | (9,852) |
| 42 | Egg Filler | (171) | (11) | 28 | | | (134) | (16) | (97) | (354) | 70 | (143) | (427) |
| 70 | Shipping & Warehousing | (269) | | 220 | | | | 86 | (68) | (31) | | 1,196 | 1,165 |
| | | 472 | (1,048) | (446) | (753) | (2,054) | (3,787) | 4,547 | (1,520) | (4,599) | 8,477 | (4,034) | (146) |

NOTE: BRACKETS ( ) ARE DEBIT COST

EXPLANATION OF SIGNIFICANT VARIANCES:

Direct Labor - Non Productive Variance - $(1,048)
  Carton Dept. - $(787)
    Training program in the die making room accounts for $(520)
    Excessive proportion on non-productive time to total time was experienced on the
    gluers due to curtailed running schedules from three shifts to two shifts
    with no change in daily and weekly cleanup time. This accounts for $(77).

Aligned Hour Variance - $(2,054)
  Too light scoring on cutting operation caused excessive reoperation costs
  of $(1,287).

Indirect Labor - $(3,787)
  Carton Dept. - $(2,174)
    The addition of three inspectors to the printing centers accounts for $(1,682).

( ) Denotes red figures

**EXHIBIT 7**

levels (viz., the plant manager, the department superintendents, and the foremen) with regard to daily and monthly performance and to provide a common ground for discussion and cooperation.

A final summary of all cost variances is prepared for each plant on the report form shown as Exhibit 8. From these statements the executive office obtains a bird's-eye view of operating effectiveness in comparison with standards. At the executive office, a cost analyst utilizes the data on these statements to prepare a statement which the president uses in his monthly report to the executive committee and board of directors.

Commenting on its plan for reporting variances, a representative of

**Summary of Cost Variances**

| CURRENT MONTH | | DESCRIPTION | YEAR TO DATE | |
|---|---|---|---|---|
| AMOUNT | % OF STD. | | AMOUNT | % OF STD. |
| | | **681  Operating Variances** | | |
| (4,589) | | 1    Direct Labor—Operating (ANALYSIS ON PAGE 2) | (39,141) | |
| (4,034) | | 2    Other Controllable Costs (ANALYSIS ON PAGE 2) | (45,376) | |
| 8,477 | | 3 .    Allowed Hour Variation (ANALYSIS ON PAGE 2) | 37,393 | |
| (146) | | | (47,124) | |
| | | **682  Service Department Variances** | | |
| (2,483) | | 1    Controllable Cost Variance (ANALYSIS ON PAGE 2) | (12,238) | |
| | | | | |
| (1,976) | | **683  Volume Variance** | | |
| | | 1    Volume Variance (ANALYSIS ON PAGE 3) | 30,935 | |
| | | **684  Material Variances (ANALYSIS ON PAGE 3)** | | |
| (1,016) | | 1    Material Price | (12,309) | |
| (535) | | 2    Material Usage | 11,795 | |
| (1,551) | | | (514) | |
| | | **685  Other Manufacturing Variances** | | |
| 5,893 | | 1    Carton Department Waste (Credit) | 50,579 | |
| | | 2 | | |
| (2,719) | | 3    Loss on Defective Finished Merchandise (Per Schedule) | (16,243) | |
| 3,174 | | | 34,336 | |
| | | **687  Inventory Adjustments** | | |
| | | 1    Adjustment to Physical | | |
| (242) | | 2    Revaluation to Market | (242) | |
| | | 3    Reclassification of Products | (1,372) | |
| (242) | | | (1,614) | |
| | | **689  Miscellaneous Cost Adjustments** | | |
| 5 | | 1    Fixed Costs (Over) or Under Budget | (8,528) | |
| (5,316) | | 2    Over or (Under) Absorbed Service Costs | (28,002) | |
| (399) | | 3    Use of Assumed Standard Product Cost | 6,139 | |
| 453 | | 4    Sale of Scrap and Junk | 4,416 | |
| (966) | | 5    Experimental Expense | (1,094) | |
| | | 6    Recoveries or Gains on Insurance Claims | 170 | |
| (1,096) | | 7    Sales and Use Taxes on Capital Additions | (13,272) | |
| | | 9    Other Miscellaneous Cost Adjustments:  (SPECIFY IN DETAIL) | | |
| 503 | | | 3,230 | |
| | | | | |
| 2,054 | | 680 )Deduct: Allowed Hour Variation Transferred to Inventory | 36,338 | |
| 711 | | 6813) | 17,413 | |
| (4,051) | | | 16,810 | |
| (7,275) | | **TOTAL COST VARIANCES** | 30,591 | |

NOTE: BRACKETS OR RED DENOTE LOSS

## EXHIBIT 8

the company stated that "We feel that we have provided to successive levels of management only the details on cost variances needed for constructive action and at a time when such action can be most effective. By integrating these reports with our regular cost accounting routine, we have been able to minimize the expense of preparing special reports and analyses."

### *Analysis of Variances By Products*

Two important purposes served by product costs are (1) to cost inventories and (2) to guide management in decisions with respect to pricing, product selection, and sales emphasis. Many of the earlier writers on standard costs believed that standard product costs should be used for these purposes and that assignment of variances to products was unnecessary. In support of this point of view, they argued that where good standards and good control practices prevailed, variance balances would be unimportant. If significant variance balances did occur, it was thought that these variances would represent losses from preventable inefficiency or temporarily depressed sales volume and that they should not be reflected in product costs.

On the other hand, most of the companies interviewed assign variances to products either regularly or occasionally. This practice is, in part at least, attributable to the impact on costs of rapid changes in prices and other conditions during recent years. Under such circumstances it has been impractical to keep standard product costs current at all times.

Most of the companies review their standard costs periodically and revise them when it is found that the standard product costs in use are no longer proper ones for the purpose. The field study shows that this revision of standard product costs usually takes place just prior to the annual closing. Up-to-date standard product costs are therefore available for costing the year-end inventory and as a basis for decisions made at that time. However, when the revised standard costs reflect anticipated manufacturing costs for the coming year which are higher than current actual costs, the valuation of the inventory should not exceed actual cost of the goods on hand at the closing date. When standard costs are revised prior to the annual closing and inventories on hand are costed at the new standard costs, the effect is, of course, to charge inventories with a part of the accumulated variances. Variances which are not considered proper inventory costs are still charged in their entirety against cost of sales for the period.

However, during the interim between periodic revisions, standard product costs are not always current. It is, of course, true that standards for material usage, operation times, and other elements of cost directly controllable by operating supervisors must be current at all times if the standards are to be satisfactory tools for cost control. These operation standards are revised when necessary without carrying changes through to the point of setting new product cost standards until the end of the year. In the meantime, differences between the operation standards and the product cost standards show as variances.

Since management usually wants current costs when decisions are to be made with respect to pricing and related questions, variances are often analyzed by products in order to arrive at current product costs. Companies producing nonstandard goods built to the customer's specifications may also analyze the variances by job orders. For such purposes the analyses are usually prepared when wanted as supplementary statistical data and are not entered in the accounts.

The analysis of variances by cause is useful in deciding whether or not current variances should be allocated to products in arriving at product costs for pricing. When management knows why the variances have occurred, it usually follows the line of reasoning expressed by H. T. McAnly in the following words:

> "If the variations represent losses which were avoidable and can be corrected, they represent definite charges against the profit or loss for the period, and cover cost—no part of which need be in future planned product cost for pricing and sales policies. If they represent revisions in values (material prices or wage rates) or insufficient unavoidable loss provisions in the planned burden, they represent adjustments which apply not only to the specific products in process during the period in which they occurred, but to the cost of all products affected by these necessary revisions.[10]

Among the companies interviewed in this study, there were several which use some or all standard costs solely to facilitate the process of computing actual costs of products. Some of these companies combine fixed standards for material prices and labor rates with current standards for other cost factors.[11] When cost control is not an objective in using standards costs and inventories are costed at historical actual cost, it is not necessary to revise standard costs when material prices and labor rates change. However, variances from such standard costs must be analyzed by products in determining current costs for managerial decisions and the variances need to be allocated between inventories and cost of goods sold when preparing financial statements.

*Examples of Variance Analysis by Products*

When analysis of variances by products is desired, suitable techniques are needed to effect the analysis without an excessive amount of clerical work. Apportionment of variances between inventories and cost of goods sold without allocation to individual products or product lines may be sufficient for financial reporting purposes. However, most of the companies charging a portion of the variances to inventories consider it necessary to analyze the variances by product classification because an overall variance ratio is not sufficiently accurate.

---

[10] "The Coming Challenge to Cost Accounting," Symposium Papers, North Carolina Association of Certified Public Accountants, 1950, p. 47.

[11] For a discussion of this procedure, see John F. Mickelson, "Standard Costs Applied to the Manufacture of Silverware," *N.A.A. Bulletin,* December 15, 1947 and James F. Merrick, "An Application of a Basic Standard Rate to Direct Labor," *N.A.A. Bulletin,* August, 1950.

Standard product costs are converted to actual costs by applying the ratio between variance balances and standard costs to the standard costs. In this process the grouping of costs and products should not be so broad as to obscure important differences in the incidence of variances on individual product classes. Examples of the procedures followed by some of the companies interviewed are given below.

*Example 1:* A comparatively small number of raw materials constitutes a major portion of the total product cost. Prices of these materials fluctuate over a wide range. For these reasons, the cost of each material is individually converted from standard to actual. On the other hand, a single percentage is used for labor and overhead combined.

*Example 2:* This company has grouped materials, basing the groupings on similarities in materials so that actual prices of the items within a group tend to fluctuate by the same percentage. To illustrate, items made of brass are in one category and items made of steel are in another category. By using ratios to fixed standard prices, clerical work required to convert standard cost to actual cost is minimized without loss of the desired accuracy.

*Example 3:* In place of deriving average adjustment factors for all items in a product line, this company first selected individual items which typify the line of products to which they belong. The standard cost of each of these items is then carefully converted to actual cost by detailed computation. Ratios between standard and actual cost of these type items are applied to standard costs of all related items. This procedure has been found quicker and clerically cheaper than the more usual method of developing overall ratios for entire product lines.

*Example 4:* The company manufactures a very wide variety of products and sales characterized by small orders. Knowledge of product profitability was stated to be the principal key to management's success in operating the business. Moreover, operations performed in each department result in a saleable commodity and inventories are carried at the various stages of manufacturing. Hence it is necessary to have a complete product cost, operation by operation. To ascertain product costs with historical job order methods would be impractical because the clerical expense would be excessive. The plan used is to issue production orders which are costed at standard cost as each operation is completed. Actual costs and standard costs are summarized monthly by operations and a single overall variance for each operation is developed. In order to determine the cost of goods sold for the monthly commodity profit and loss statement, shipments are first summarized by commodities and extended at standard cost. The appropriate variance ratios are then applied to the standard cost figures to obtain the actual cost of each commodity sold.

## Conclusion

Variances serve to direct management's attention to the fact that current costs have deviated from standard costs. While cost control must be exercised before the fact and variances are ascertained after the fact, prompt review of variance history can bring to light conditions needing attention and it can also provide management with information which contributes to the making of sounder decisions with respect to the future.

Since costs are controlled by individuals, determining responsibility for variances is the first step toward making variance data useful for cost control. Accumulation of standard and actual costs controllable by each managerial responsibility in the company's organization provides a measure of managerial performance in comparison with the standards established for the purpose.

Before intelligent action based upon variance information can be taken, it is necessary to know why the variances arose. Hence analysis to determine the causes of variances makes the variance data more useful. Analyses by cause may be made regularly according to a preestablished procedure or they may be made by special studies in which the methods and objectives differ from one study to another. Examples of both of these approaches have been given in earlier pages of this report. Most companies make some use of both approaches.

While much may be learned by a well directed analysis of variances, the ultimate value of the analysis rests upon effective communication of the results to managerial personnel. Reports which bring out the significance of variance data in terms of the problems faced by executives and supervisors are useful for the purpose. However, experience shows that reports need to be accompanied by the informal methods of communication which develop when the accountant works closely with operating management. In small companies, the latter methods largely replace formal reports.

For such purposes as pricing, management wants current product costs which include all costs which it aims to recover in selling prices. Where standard costs are current and variances are relatively small, analysis of variances by products may be unnecessary. Nevertheless, the field study shows that it is often impractical to maintain standard product costs which are continuously current or to eliminate variances from standards which are based upon preferred methods and materials, normal variety, and similar conditions. Hence most of the companies interviewed analyze variances by products before using the costs as guides to decisions with respect to pricing and product selection.

On the other hand, the common practice of revising standard costs at the end of the year provides up-to-date standard product costs for costing the year-end inventory. Consequently, assignment of variances to products for this purpose is usually not considered necessary.

# THE CALCULATION OF VARIANCES

Variances from direct costs are caused by deviations from the projected quantities of materials incorporated in the standards and also by deviations from the projected prices for these materials, which have also been incorporated in the standards. It is assumed that price and quantity are the only two variables present, and this assumption is implicit in the method of computation of these direct cost variances.

### Computation of Price and Quantity Variance

A price variance, as usually determined in practice, may be stated as the difference between standard and actual unit price times the *actual* number of units purchased. The quantity variance is then calculated as the difference between standard and actual quantities times the *standard* price per unit. The following figures illustrate the computations.

| | |
|---|---|
| Standard price per unit | $ 1.00 |
| Actual price per unit | 1.10 |
| Standard quantity | 100 units |
| Actual quantity | 120 units |
| Price variance ($1.00 minus $1.10 times 120 units) | 12.00 |
| Quantity variance (100 units minus 120 units times $1.00) | 20.00 |
| Total variance ($100 minus $132) | $32.00 |

However, when the problem of calculating these variances is viewed solely from the mathematical standpoint, there are alternative methods of calculation which yield different results. For example, price and quantity variances could be calculated as follows:

| | |
|---|---|
| Price variance ($1.00 minus $1.10 times 100 units) | $10.00 |
| Quantity variance (100 units minus 120 units times $1.10) | 22.00 |
| Total variance | $32.00 |

In fact, an application of mathematical analysis alone leads to the conclusion that the total variance traceable to price alone can be determined only when no quantity variance is present. Likewise, the "pure" quantity variance can be determined only in the absence of a price variance. Whenever both actual price and actual quantity differ from the corresponding standards, a

38

portion of the overall variance (i.e., the combined price and quantity variance) is a joint product of price and quantity differences. A diagram illustrating the above statements is shown as Exhibit 1.

In this diagram, area D is the joint result of price and quantity variances. Just as it is not possible to say what part of the area of a rectangle is ascribable

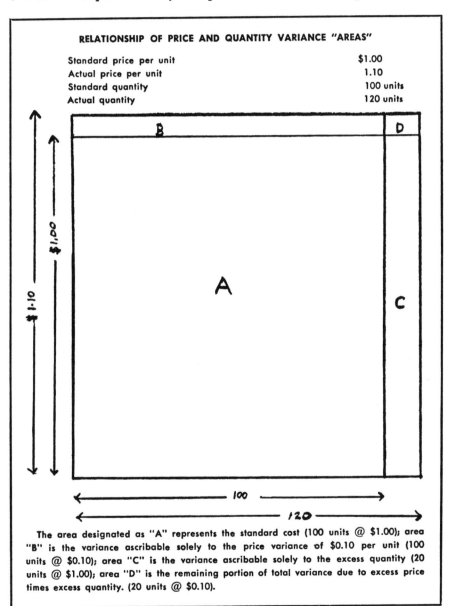

**RELATIONSHIP OF PRICE AND QUANTITY VARIANCE "AREAS"**

| | |
|---|---|
| Standard price per unit | $1.00 |
| Actual price per unit | 1.10 |
| Standard quantity | 100 units |
| Actual quantity | 120 units |

The area designated as "A" represents the standard cost (100 units @ $1.00); area "B" is the variance ascribable solely to the price variance of $0.10 per unit (100 units @ $0.10); area "C" is the variance ascribable solely to the excess quantity (20 units @ $1.00); area "D" is the remaining portion of total variance due to excess price times excess quantity. (20 units @ $0.10).

**EXHIBIT 1**

to length and what part to height, it is impossible to say that any portion of the joint variance amounting to $2.00 is caused by either price or quantity by itself.

The first method of computing variances illustrated above includes area D with area B to make up the price variance. The second method combines area D with area C to form the quantity variance. Still another method has been suggested by a writer on the subject who proposes that area D be divided between the price and quantity variances.[1]

The mathematical logic underlying variance computations offers no guidance in choosing from the possible alternatives in disposition of the joint product of the two variances—i.e., area D. Instead, the answer must be sought by asking what method yields information most useful to management.

The cost accountant's primary objective in computing variances is to provide management with information which is useful in controlling costs. This objective is best accomplished by measuring variances in terms of responsibilities rather than in terms of cost factors such as price and quantity. As expressed by a member of the Committee on Research:

> "One of the failings of the so-called 'actual' cost systems was that by prorating all costs back to the operating department, controllable and non-controllable costs were so intermingled that the operator could be held responsible for very little of them.

> "If we are to accept the principle that an operator should be held responsible only for those variances which are under his control, there can be only one answer. One of the fundamentals of the responsibility type of standard cost accounting is that each responsibility head shall be charged for the materials and services which he uses at a standard cost. No variances are transferred from any anterior department or process. This guarantees that he will be held responsible only for the variances arising from his own operations. In the example given, therefore, it is my opinion that quantity variance should be only the excess units over standard used times their standard value. To charge the operator with any of the price variance on the extra units used would introduce an element over which he has no control."

Those individuals in the organization who are responsible for exercising control over the quantity of materials used are not ordinarily responsible for the unit price paid for the material. Placement of responsibility for cost control therefore requires a dollar quantity variance which is directly proportional to the physical units of material in the quantity variance. This is accomplished by extending the physical quantities by the standard unit price.[2] Similarly, management in charge of the purchasing function does not

---

[1] See Lawrence L. Vance, "The Fundamental Logic of Primary Variance Analysis," *N.A.A. Bulletin*, January 1950.

[2] This relationship is not maintained by use of any other price. For example, using the second method illustrated above in which the physical quantity variance is multiplied by the actual unit price, the dollar quantity variance changes when the actual price paid for the material changes, even though the quantity excess remains the same.

control the quantity of material used, and to the extent that responsibility can be placed for the price of materials purchased, this responsibility is limited to the unit price paid. Hence the significant price variance is the difference between standard and actual unit prices and the total amount of this variance depends upon the number of units actually purchased.

Occasionally, circumstances may arise in which the above described method does not bring all of the facts needed to establish responsibility for variances. For example, one company found that excess usage of materials not carried in stock required additional purchases at premium prices. Moreover, there had been frequent use of the company's toolroom to manufacture component parts when stocks were exhausted by excess spoilage. Here the real cost of the quantity variances was substantially increased by paying higher prices for materials needed to complete orders or to meet promised delivery dates. When this situation was brought to management's attention, a program to reduce waste and spoilage of materials was instituted. While situations such as this do not mean that customary methods for computing price and quantity variances need to be changed, they indicate that there is need for study to ascertain the basic facts that underlie variances.

## Overhead Variances

The total overhead cost variance measures the difference between standard overhead cost absorbed by production and the actual amount of overhead cost incurred during the period. Its analysis is more complicated than the analysis of variances from direct costs, since it entails consideration of volume as a third variable, in addition to price and quantity which are the two variables present in direct cost analysis. The overall variance is ordinarily broken down into two or three separate variances. However, different methods for determining these overhead variances are to be found in the literature and in practice. These methods and the differences among them are described below.

## Primary Overhead Variance Components

Methods for determining overhead variances make use of four primary components which are combined in different ways to produce two or three variances. These components are not computed separately in practice, but they underlie the methods used and are basic to an understanding of the differences between the various methods. Terms used below to designate the variance components have been coined for descriptive purposes.

A. "Budget controllable component," due to spending more (or less) than the amount allowed by the flexible budget for the actual man or machine hours. This variance is calculated as the difference between the amount of expense budgeted for the actual man or machine hours and the actual amount of expense incurred during the period.

B. "Excess hours controllable component," or the excess (or saving) in variable cost incurred because actual hours exceed (or are less than) the standard hours. This variance component is the difference between overhead cost allowed for the number of standard man or machine hours and the overhead cost allowed for the number of actual hours.

C. "Excess hours volume component," or the amount of fixed cost underabsorbed (or overabsorbed) due to use of more (or fewer) hours than standard for the volume of production attained during the period. This component can be calculated as the difference between the amount of fixed cost applied to production (i.e., standard hours produced times a rate based upon budgeted cost for standard or normal volume) and the amount of standard fixed cost applicable to the actual number of man or machine hours.

D. "Capacity volume component," or the amount of fixed cost underabsorbed (or overabsorbed) because the number of actual man or machine hours falls short of (or is greater than) the standard or normal capacity, measured in hours. This component can be calculated as the difference between total standard fixed cost for the period and the amount of standard fixed cost applicable to the actual hours.

The derivation of the above components is illustrated by means of a diagram and numerical example in Exhibit 2. For purposes of the example, the following data are assumed.

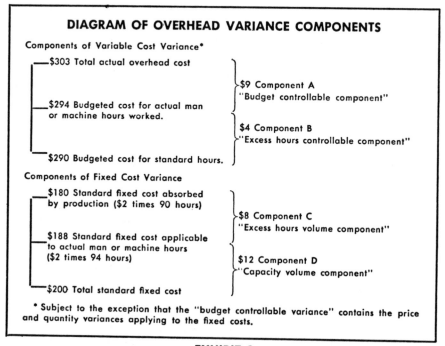

## DIAGRAM OF OVERHEAD VARIANCE COMPONENTS

Components of Variable Cost Variance*

—$303 Total actual overhead cost

$9 Component A
"Budget controllable component"

—$294 Budgeted cost for actual man or machine hours worked.

$4 Component B
"Excess hours controllable component"

—$290 Budgeted cost for standard hours.

Components of Fixed Cost Variance

—$180 Standard fixed cost absorbed by production ($2 times 90 hours)

$8 Component C
"Excess hours volume component"

—$188 Standard fixed cost applicable to actual man or machine hours ($2 times 94 hours)

$12 Component D
"Capacity volume component"

—$200 Total standard fixed cost

* Subject to the exception that the "budget controllable variance" contains the price and quantity variances applying to the fixed costs.

**EXHIBIT 2**

42

Flexible overhead cost standards:
Fixed cost, per month ................................................................................. $200
Variable cost, per standard hour ........................................................... $ 1
Standard (or normal) volume, in standard hours per month ................ 100
Standard overhead rate, per standard hour:
Fixed component, $200/100 hours ................................................ $2
Variable component, per standard hour ........................................ 1 $ 3

Actual overhead cost incurred for month ................................................ $303
Actual man or machine hours in month ................................................. 94
Standard hours allowed for production during month ........................... 90

## Analysis Plans Using Two Variances

The field studies show that most companies using standard costs develop two overhead variances. These are generally called *controllable variance* and *volume variance.*[3] The controllable variance is made up of components A and B described above, while the volume variance includes components C and D. Computation of these variances, using the above, follows:

"Normal" production volume per month 100 Standard Hours

Actual overhead expense for month ........................................................ $303
Expense allowed for standard hours produced:
Fixed .................................................................................................... $200
Variable (90 hours @ $1) ................................................................. 90 290

Controllable Variance $ 13

Overhead expense allowed for standard hours produced:
Fixed .................................................................................................... $200
Variable (90 hours @ $1) ................................................................. 90 $290

Overhead expense absorbed by production:
Standard rate is $300/100 or $3 (90 hours @ $3) ........................ 270

Volume variance $ 20

Determination of the two variances ordinarily accompanies the use of a flexible budget which permits calculation of expense allowances for various volumes within the range of fluctuation normally expected, although these two variances may be calculated from a fixed budget when circumstances justify its use. If all units produced in the cost center are identical, volume may be measured in terms of number of units. Since this is usually not the case, volume is ordinarily measured in man hours for man operation cost centers and in machine hours for machine operation cost centers.

If hours are used, volume should be measured in standard hours, not in actual hours. This follows from the fact that standard hours are directly proportional to physical units produced in a cost center while the ratio of actual hours to physical units fluctuates. In other words, an increase in the actual hours required for a given quantity of production, in the absence of other variables, indicates decreased efficiency, not increased volume. In practice, volume is sometimes approximated by adding a small portion of

---

[3] This method is described by Reitell and Harris, "Cost Accounting," published by International Textbook Co., 1948.

43

actual or estimated hours to standard hours because it may not be economically justifiable to standardize 100% of the production. Standard labor dollars are directly proportional to physical production when standard labor rates are constant within a man operation cost center and the desired production volume statistics are often more easily accumulated in terms of labor dollars.

The volume variance consists of standard fixed cost dollars over or under absorbed while the controllable variance includes cost differences arising from operation of all other variables. This includes any differences between the actual and budgeted amounts for fixed expenses. However, the controllable variance is primarily a measure of differences between the amount of variable expense allowed in the flexible budget for the number of standard hours produced and the actual amount of variable expense incurred.

Where direct labor is included with overhead and applied to production at a combined rate, the above variances include direct labor variances.

The controllable variance is broken down by departments corresponding to responsibilities, and for each responsibility, variances are determined for each item of expense (e.g., supplies, indirect labor, etc.). The latter are differences between the amount of expense allowed for the number of standard hours produced and the actual overhead costs for the period. Further analysis to determine causes of variances for individual expense items can be made if desired.

One company interviewed in the field study separates component B (i.e., the excess variable expense ascribable to using more than the standard number of hours to manufacture the number of pieces produced) because this makes clear the fact that efforts to control the variance must be directed toward avoiding excess direct labor rather than toward the overhead expenses themselves. The company representative pointed out that such control is important because savings in variable overhead as well as in direct labor mean direct savings in out-of-pocket cash expenditures.

## Analysis Plans Using Three Variances

While less common in practice than the use of two overhead variances, a few companies develop three overhead variances. Such plans are often described in cost accounting textbooks.

The use of three overhead variances isolates the effect of differences between actual and standard hours on fixed of variable costs or both. It therefore seems that a plan employing three overhead variances would be more useful than a two variance plan only where there are frequent and important differences between actual hours and standard hours and where these differences are not more conveniently controllable by other means.

The three variances are obtained by combining the previously described

# TABULAR SUMMARY OF OVERHEAD VARIANCE ANALYSIS METHODS

| TWO VARIANCE METHODS | PRIMARY COMPONENTS | THREE VARIANCE METHODS — Method 1 | Method 2 | Method 3 |
|---|---|---|---|---|
| Controllable Variance (A + B) | A—Budget Controllable Component—Actual burden dollars for month less flexible budget allowance for standard hours corresponding to actual hours used for actual production in month. | First Variance (A) | First Variance (A + B) | First Variance (A) |
| | B—Excess Hours Controllable Component—Flexible budget allowance for standard hours corresponding to actual hours used for actual production in month less flexible budget allowance for standard hours allowed for actual production in month. | Second Variance (B) | | Second Variance (B + C) |
| Volume Variance (C + D) | C—Excess Hours Volume Component — Fixed component of standard burden rate times difference of actual less standard hours for actual production in the month. | Third Variance (C + D) | Second Variance (C) | |
| | D—Capacity Volume Component — Fixed component of standard burden rate times difference of "normal" hours for the month less actual hours for the month. | | Third Variance (D) | Third Variance (D) |

Total Variance (A+B+C+D)

**EXHIBIT 3**

45

components in three different ways. These are described below and summarized in Exhibit 3. Figures used are taken from Exhibit 2.

*Method 1:* Components A and B are treated as separate variances, but components C and D are combined into a single volume variance.[4]

| | |
|---|---|
| First variance (A) | $ 9 |
| Second variance (B) | 4 |
| Third variance, (C plus D) | 20 |
| | |
| Total variance | $33 |

It seems that this method might be the most useful of the three variance plans when variable overhead costs are high in relation to fixed costs, or it is otherwise desired to focus attention on variances from variable costs.

*Method 2:* Components A and B are combined into a single variance while components C and D are shown as separate variances.[5]

| | |
|---|---|
| First variance (A plus B) | $13 |
| Second variance (C) | 8 |
| Third variance (D) | 12 |
| | |
| Total variance | $33 |

This method tends to focus attention on the fixed costs and would probably be preferable to method 1 when fixed overhead costs are high relative to variable overhead costs.

*Method 3:* Components B and C are combined into one variance while components A and D are reported as separate variances.[6]

| | |
|---|---|
| First variance (A) | $ 9 |
| Second variance (B plus C) | 12 |
| Third variance (D) | 12 |
| | |
| | $33 |

These variances might constitute a useful analysis when the plant operates steadily at a volume close enough to standard capacity so fixed and variable costs of the excess hours may reasonably be combined to show a total cost for excess hours, i.e., when the fixed costs corresponding to the excess hours could have been used for extra production instead of being lost as idle capacity.

---

[4] Described by J. H. March, "Cost Accounting," published by McGraw-Hill Book Company, 1949.

[5] Described by Uniform Accounting Manual for Electrical Manufacturing Industry, 1950.

[6] Described by C. F. Schlatter, "Cost Accounting," published by John Wiley & Sons, Inc., 1947.

## LIST OF COMPANIES PARTICIPATING IN STUDY

The following companies were among those participating in this NAA Research Study by contributing information regarding their methods. The remaining companies preferred that their names not be listed.

ACME STEEL COMPANY
AMERICAN HARD RUBBER COMPANY
AMERICAN MACHINE & FOUNDRY
COMPANY
AMERICAN TYPE FOUNDERS, INC.
ANACONDA WIRE AND CABLE
COMPANY
BRISTOL-MYERS COMPANY
BLACK & DECKER MFG. CO.
CELOTEX CORPORATION
CIBA PHARMACEUTICAL PRODUCTS
CURTIS LIGHTING, INC.
DAVISON CHEMICAL CORPORATION
THOMAS A. EDISON, INCORPORATED

FIBREBOARD PRODUCTS, INC.
HYATT BEARINGS DIVISION, GENERAL
MOTORS CORPORATION
INTERNATIONAL RESISTANCE
COMPANY
JOHNSON & JOHNSON
G. KRUEGER BREWING COMPANY
MONROE CALCULATING MACHINE
COMPANY
NASH ENGINEERING COMPANY
SCHERING CORPORATION
SYLVANIA ELECTRIC PRODUCTS, INC.
R. WALLACE & SONS MFG. CO.